THRIVING WOMEN

WITH

ADHD

Transform Your Life — A Simple DBT Workbook to Master Emotional Regulation, Enhance Executive Functioning, Ignite Emotional Intelligence, and Celebrate Your Neurodiversity

SpreadLife
Publishing

Thriving Women with ADHD

Transform Your Life — A Simple DBT Workbook to Master Emotional Regulation, Enhance Executive Functioning, Ignite Emotional Intelligence, and Celebrate Your Neurodiversity

By SpreadLife Publishing

a result of the use of the information contained within this document, including, but not limited to, errors, omissions, or inaccuracies.

Download the Audiobook Version for FREE

If you love listening to audiobooks on the go,

you can download the audiobook version of this book for FREE (regularly $19.95)

just by signing up for a FREE 30-day Audible trial!

Click one of the links below to get started.

>> For Audible US <<

>> For Audible UK <<

>> For Audible FR <<

>> For Audible DE <<

Contents

Conclusion 202

Resources 206

Introction

Kate sat on her doorstep with a pounding headache. The acrid smell of burnt toast hung heavy in the air. Again. She'd meant to keep an eye on breakfast while she helped Henry with his math, but one minute she was explaining long division and the next, the kitchen was covered in smoke.

She heard Tom coming out of the house, his brow furrowed in concern. "Another one?" he asked, his voice a mix of exasperation and pity. Kate tried to smile, but it felt forced. She knew the look. The look that said, "I told you so." And he had. Countless times.

Inside, Nathan was wailing. He probably tripped over his toys. Kate groaned. The day was barely past dawn, and already, she was at her wits' end. She should be at work; she couldn't afford to miss another deadline. Her boss's icy tone from the previous day echoed in her ears. He had threatened to fire her—and that would be fair. Every day, she was either late, fighting with her coworkers, or way behind schedule on her projects.

Kate ran a hand through her tangled hair, the headache throbbing. She was tired of being seen as incompetent. She was intelligent, capable, even brilliant at times. But the ADHD was a relentless undertow, pulling her down just when she thought she was treading water.

She glanced at the clock. Late. The world outside was a blur of colors and sounds; everything moved too fast. She needed to escape, to find a quiet corner where she could focus, just for a moment. But there was no escape. Not today.

What would a monochromatic world look like? That would mean a world totally devoid of colors. Just shades of black, white, and gray. Quite boring, right? Blue is my favorite color—not just one shade of blue, but every possible hue. I cannot imagine a world without the blue skies or my favorite navy blue chunky sweater that keeps me warm in the frigid winter.

So, back to my question. A monochromatic world would mean gray skies, the streets full of white cars, and maybe all the flowers would be black. Weird, right? Can you take a minute to try to imagine a world where everyone thought the same way, judged things exactly the same way, and maybe even dressed exactly the same way? We would all be like a bunch of zombies, don't you think?

That's kind of what it's like when we don't acknowledge our neurodiversity, let alone allowing ourselves to express it. Neurodiversity challenges the way we think about who "fits in" and what a "normal" brain is. Neurodiversity means recognizing that brains are wired differently, and that's a good thing. It asks us to see differences as strengths, not something to be hidden. Think of all the cool inventions or creative solutions that might never have existed if everyone thought the same way. I mean, just take a look at how many ways eggs can be prepared. If we all agreed that hard-boiled eggs were the "normal" way to eat eggs, we would never have scrambled eggs or omelets.

In a world that often tries to put people in boxes, neurodiversity shows us the potential for a society that's more inclusive and dynamic—and way more interesting. One of the best things about neurodiversity is that it focuses on what people are good at, not what they struggle with. Opening your heart up to your neurodiversity helps you accept all that you are (creativity, femininity, quirks, and all).

I have worked with women like Kate over the years, and I definitely cannot deny the incredible strength of femininity. It's a force that is robust, intuitive, and strong all at once. It breaks my heart to see women consistently living below their potential, burdened by the weight of societal expectations and misunderstandings about their neurodivergent brains.

You can see this strength portrayed in how women are both diverse and adaptable. Women have an innate ability to connect, empathize, and love in ways that sometimes can't be described with words. When combined with the traits of ADHD—such as creativity, hyperfocus, and a super strong will—this strength becomes a formidable asset. For example, when you combine creativity and hyperfocus, you get someone who can stay focused on a project for hours and come up with something incredibly wonderful.

Yet, too often, women with ADHD are told to fit into boxes that were never designed with their brilliance in mind. They are pressured to conform to standards that stifle their true potential. This constant battle to fit in can be exhausting and disheartening.

It's like trying to force a round peg into a square hole. It just doesn't fit. It pains me to see so many women undervaluing their potential, believing they are less-than because they don't fit the mold. The truth is, the world needs the unique gifts that neurodivergent women bring. It needs their innovation, their different way of thinking, and their ability to see connections that others might miss.

This workbook is designed to help you tap into that strength and unleash your full potential. I will show you how you can break free from societal pressures and redefine what success looks like for you.

That will help you build a life that is not only fulfilling but also true to who you are.

You must be strong, resilient, and willing to accept and enjoy your neurodiversity. You'll also need a thick skin to question deeply entrenched societal standards. Sure, you'll have moments of doubt and hardship, but these are the times that shape your growth and strengthen your spirit. These difficulties reveal your genuine strength and ability.

Why is it worth it? This is your chance to live fully and well. With your unique abilities and viewpoints, you create a world of possibilities for yourself and the people around you. Your road to self-discovery and empowerment has the potential to inspire and drive change, paving the way for a more inclusive and understanding society. You deserve a life in which you are respected for who you truly are. Moreover, the world needs your intelligence, creativity, and unique perspectives.

So, come along with me on this journey. Take each step (or chapter) with confidence and hope, knowing that it will lead to greater self-awareness, fulfillment, and long-term impact.

I assure you that as you work through the exercises and reflections, you will get to see that your femininity and neurodiversity are not obstacles. They are your greatest strengths. They are what make you unique and valuable.

Let me close this "welcoming" with one of my favorite quotes of all time. It was originally written by Marianne Williamson, but I came across it while watching *Akeelah and the Bee*. Either way, here it goes:

"Our deepest fear is not that we are inadequate. Our deepest fear is that we are powerful beyond measure. It is our light, not our darkness, that most

frightens us. We ask ourselves, 'Who am I to be brilliant, gorgeous, talented, fabulous?' Actually, who are you not to be?

"*You are a child of God. Your playing small does not serve the world. There is nothing enlightened about shrinking so that other people won't feel insecure around you. We are all meant to shine, as children do.*

"*We were born to manifest the glory of God that is within us. It's not just in some of us; it's in everyone. And as we let our own light shine, we unconsciously give other people permission to do the same. As we are liberated from our own fear, our presence automatically liberates others.*"

So, shake off the stereotypes. We're about to change the narrative.

PART ONE

Understanding and Embracing ADHD

Knowing you have ADHD is the first step. It helps you understand why you find some stuff hard, like paying attention, keeping things tidy, or holding yourself back. Once you know it's ADHD causing this, you can find ways to make things easier.

Accepting ADHD doesn't mean there's something wrong with you. It's just part of who you are. It's like having blue eyes or brown hair. And guess what? It doesn't have to stop you from doing the things you want to do.

CHAPTER ONE

Embrace Your Mind

"Nobody is wired wrong because there's no wrong and right in the way we are."

—Hannah Hart

"I will praise You, for I am fearfully and wonderfully made; Marvelous are Your works, And that my soul knows very well."

—Psalms 139:14 (NKJV)

Case Study

My last haircut got me pretty excited. Not because of the potential new 'do, but because I'd finally found a stylist who could handle my constant chatter. It felt so good to be able to talk fast and jump from topic to topic without being given the side eye.

Growing up, I was that kid you would tag "troublesome." The one labeled a tomboy because climbing trees and building forts was more appealing than playing with dolls. I was always on the go, and I sure wore my mother out. Little did I know that all of these were a precursor to something bigger.

As I got older, hanging out with friends got harder. I didn't get all the rules about how to act. And I talked a lot! People would say, "Wow, you never *stop talking!" But inside my head, it felt like there were a million things I wanted to say.*

Even though I liked to talk, I hated going to parties. Too many people, too much noise, it made me feel shy and overwhelmed. And when I talked to people, my mind would wander off if I wasn't the one talking or if it wasn't something I really liked.

—*Linda*

Maybe you're like Linda. You've felt different for as long as you can remember. Like a puzzle piece that just doesn't quite fit. You've been told you're too much, too loud, too disorganized. I totally get that. But there's a reason for that. It's not because you're flawed, but because your brain works differently. It's time to stop feeling like an outsider and start understanding the incredible mind you possess. And maybe it's a little comforting to know that millions of women are in the same boat with you.

Knowing how your mind works helps you understand yourself. This helps you figure out what works for you and what doesn't. I know it's hard to deal with ADHD, but it's even harder when you keep fighting yourself. Before the world can accept you, you need to accept yourself and all that you are—and not only that, but be kind to yourself.

The Science of ADHD

What were your first thoughts the first time you heard about ADHD? Did you brush it off as just another invention to explain away your symptoms? Or did you go online and google all possible information, good and not so good, you could lay your hands on? My good friend Anne told me she felt a mix of relief and skepticism when she found out about ADHD. She had always been labeled the "daydreamer" or the one who couldn't sit still, and now there was a name for it. But she wondered, could ADHD really explain everything?

ADHD, or attention deficit hyperactivity disorder, is a condition that affects how the brain functions, particularly in areas related to focus, impulse control, and organization. ADHD is often misunderstood as simply being "distracted" or "hyperactive." You've probably been guilt tripped and made to feel that it's all your fault. But the truth is that you have no control over the way your brain is wired. Just as you can't determine whether you're blonde or red-haired at birth, you can't decide whether or not you want to develop ADHD.

ADHD is a condition that stems from the way our brains are wired. There is still ongoing research as to exactly what causes it, but discoveries have been made. One key area of focus is the brain's structure itself. Studies have shown that the brains of people with ADHD look a bit different from those without it (Rubia, 2018). For example, the prefrontal cortex (which is like the brain's command center) is smaller or less active in people with ADHD. This is the part of the brain that helps you pay attention, make plans, and make decisions. It's not hard to see why it may be a bit difficult to focus, plan, and decide on things with ADHD.

Let me go a little further. Neurotransmitters are chemical messengers that relay information between brain cells. This is sort of like a relay race with batons passed from one runner to another. Dopamine and norepinephrine are two key neurotransmitters implicated in ADHD. These chemicals help you pay attention, focus, and process rewards. In ADHD, the batons are either not passed at all or the receiving athlete drops the baton. This creates an imbalance in these neurotransmitters, leading to difficulties with attention, impulsivity, and hyperactivity.

While not the primary cause, environmental factors can also influence the expression of ADHD symptoms. These factors include prenatal exposure to toxins or substances, traumatic experiences, or adverse childhood events. For example, a child exposed to high levels of stress or instability at home might develop symptoms similar to ADHD, especially if such a child already has genetic inclination towards ADHD.

ADHD in Women (The Unique Presentation)

The symptoms of ADHD in women often present differently compared to in men. In women, symptoms tend to be more subtle and internalized, and may even manifest as primarily inattentive rather than the more common hyperactive-impulsive. Moreover, emotional regulation difficulties, including mood swings and intense emotional responses, can be prominent. Social interactions can also be impacted, with women struggling to understand social cues and maintain relationships. Tough, right?

Interestingly, many women develop coping strategies to mask ADHD symptoms. This can lead to burnout and increased stress. Physical symptoms like restlessness, insomnia, and chronic fatigue can also come up. Furthermore, ADHD in women is frequently diagnosed later in life, making recognition and treatment more challenging.

Several factors contribute to these distinct manifestations. Societal expectations and gender roles, for example, have a way of shaping how ADHD symptoms are perceived and expressed in women. Hormonal fluctuations can also influence how severe these symptoms are as well as how they present. Differences in brain structure or function between genders also contribute to the disparity.

Historically, a diagnostic bias towards ADHD in boys has led to underdiagnosis in women. Most people tend to pick up hyperactivity in boys earlier. Consequently, coping mechanisms developed by women to manage ADHD symptoms differ from those employed by men, impacting the overall experience. Another factor that affects this presentation is the intersection of ADHD with other mental health conditions, which can further complicate symptom presentation in women.

Let me expand more on societal expectations. Traditional gender roles usually portray women as organized, multitasking, and emotionally stable. I remember watching *The Smurfs* in the 1980s; Smurfette was the only female in the whole village. She was the one who kept everyone in line while the male Smurfs were off on adventures. It's crazy to think how these subtle messages can stick with you.

These stereotypes create a stark contrast with the common ADHD symptoms of difficulty focusing, disorganization, and emotional regulation challenges. As a result, women with ADHD feel immense pressure to conform to these expectations, leading to feelings of inadequacy and low self-esteem. Can you relate?

The discrepancy between societal norms and the realities of ADHD can make these symptoms even worse and also contribute to mental health issues. For instance, when you internalize your struggles, you blame yourself and see yourself as inadequate rather than dealing with the real culprit—ADHD. Moreover, the pressure to do well in multiple areas, such as your career, family, and social life, can be overwhelming, increasing risk of burnout.

There are also societal misconceptions about ADHD, which are rooted in the more prevalent hyperactive-impulsive presentation in boys. Often, people interpret ADHD as the stereotypical "doing too much." This notion also leads to underdiagnosis and misdiagnosis in women. This lack of recognition can delay access to appropriate support and treatment, prolonging the impact of ADHD on women's lives.

When you struggle with things like focusing, getting organized, or controlling your emotions and don't understand why, it's easy to blame yourself. It feels like everyone else can manage, but you can't, and that's a huge hit to your self-esteem.

On top of that, trying to deal with ADHD without the right tools makes things even more difficult. It can lead to feeling anxious or depressed. And because it's harder to make and keep friends when you have ADHD, you might end up feeling lonely too. To make things worse, without a diagnosis, women with ADHD often push themselves really hard to cope. They might try to be perfect or work nonstop, which can lead to burnout and other problems.

It's also harder to get the support you need. Things like therapy, medication, or time management techniques can make a huge difference, but you can't access them if you don't know what's going on.

And let's not forget the impact on relationships. ADHD can make it harder to connect with people, both personally and professionally. Without a diagnosis, it's even tougher to understand and manage these challenges. Basically, underdiagnosis can create a ripple effect of problems that make life harder than it needs to be.

Hormonal Influences on ADHD Throughout a Woman's Life

Hormones influence everything from physical development to emotional well-being. Estrogen and progesterone are primary female hormones, and they work together to regulate the menstrual cycle, bone formation, and even mood.

Hormonal fluctuations, however, can lead to a range of factors such as physical discomfort and menstrual irregularities. These experiences, while normal, can affect a woman's quality of life. Rising and falling hormones during the menstrual cycle can worsen ADHD symptoms, especially when estrogen levels are low. Common issues include increased impulsivity, difficulty focusing, and mood swings.

Pregnancy and postpartum also come with dramatic hormone shifts. These changes can exacerbate ADHD symptoms, leading to memory problems, difficulty concentrating, and emotional volatility. Estrogen levels rise significantly during pregnancy and then plummet after childbirth. These rapid changes affect dopamine and serotonin levels.

Beyond the direct impact on ADHD symptoms, the demands of pregnancy and postpartum can create additional issues. Pregnancy-related discomfort and newborn care can disrupt sleep, further affecting concentration and mood. The physical and emotional demands of motherhood can contribute to heightened stress levels, which can worsen ADHD symptoms.

Let's not forget menopause. Menopause can be regarded as a natural decline in reproductive hormones when a woman reaches her forties or fifties. The start of menopause is signaled by 12 months without menstruation. Estrogen levels come down during menopause, which can result in worsened ADHD symptoms, including memory issues, trouble focusing, and increased anxiety or depression.

However, I need to mention that not all women with ADHD experience serious hormonal impacts. The severity of the effects varies from person to person.

Myths and Facts

I love to play two truths and a lie with my friends. It's a fun way to test your knowledge and perception, and it often reveals surprising misconceptions. This got me thinking about the countless myths and facts that circulate in our daily lives. From ancient folklore to modern-day misinformation, it can be hard to distinguish between what's real and what's imagined. Let me dispel some myths about ADHD. I'll share common misconceptions followed by the facts

Myth: ADHD is just for boys.

- **Fact:** While ADHD is more often diagnosed in boys, it affects women too. However, symptoms can come up in different ways in women, making it harder to recognize.

Myth: Women with ADHD are just disorganized or lazy.

- **Fact:** ADHD is a neurodevelopmental disorder, not a personality flaw. Women with ADHD have issues with attention, focus, and impulsivity, just like men.

Myth: Growing up means growing out of ADHD.

- **Fact:** You may be able to manage your symptoms better, but ADHD sometimes goes on into adulthood. And in some cases, some women don't realize they have ADHD until later in life.

Myth: Medication is the only treatment for ADHD.

- **Fact:** While medication can be helpful, it's not the sole treatment. I'll be sharing many effective management strategies in the coming chapters.

Myth: ADHD is caused by poor parenting.

- **Fact:** ADHD is a neurological condition, not a result of bad parenting. Could your parents have helped in managing your symptoms better? Maybe. But could they have caused you to develop ADHD? Definitely not.

Myth: ADHD is caused by sugar or food additives.

- **Fact:** While diet can influence behavior and focus, there's no scientific evidence linking specific foods to ADHD.

Myth: Women with ADHD are less intelligent than those without it.

- **Fact:** ADHD doesn't affect intelligence. Many people with ADHD are highly intelligent.

Neurodiversity: Embracing Different Wiring

Let's talk about something fascinating: our brains. Just like we all have different eye colors, our brains are all wired uniquely and work in different ways. This is what we call neurodiversity.

Neurodiversity includes conditions like ADHD, autism, dyslexia, and dyspraxia. I need you to see beyond the stereotypes of these conditions; they are simply different ways of thinking and learning. People with these conditions have incredible strengths and offer unique perspectives.

However, let's be honest, it's not always easy. Social situations, sensory overload, and planning can be tough for some. But just like brown eyes, blue eyes, and green eyes are equally beautiful, so are our differently wired brains. We need to create a world where everyone feels valued and supported, regardless of how their brain works.

People with neurodiverse brains may be exceptional at pattern recognition, problem-solving, or creative thinking. They process information differently, and thus might need different teaching methods. There is also the tendency to have stronger focus in specific areas. Neurodiverse women can be incredibly passionate and knowledgeable about particular subjects.

While neurodiversity offers unique strengths, it also comes with its unique difficulties. People with neurodiverse brains might face difficulties with understanding social cues and expectations. They may also find overwhelming environments quite stressful.

The Diagnosis Journey: Why So Many Women Are Overlooked

It is frustrating to be treated as though you are invisible, and there is also the sheer exhaustion that comes from being overlooked. It's unacceptable. Your experiences, your perspectives, and your contributions are valid. I know that words alone won't erase the countless instances of being dismissed, underestimated, or simply ignored. Even more heartbreaking is the fact that the health system is not excluded from this disparity. In fact, the disparities in healthcare are a prime example of this systemic issue. It's a disgrace that women's health concerns have often been relegated to the sidelines of medical research. But there's a growing awareness, and we're pushing for change.

Like I mentioned earlier, ADHD in women often presents with more subtle symptoms, like difficulty focusing, organizing, and managing emotions. These aren't as noticeable as the hyperactive behavior often associated with ADHD in males. Because of these subtle symptoms, women are often misdiagnosed with conditions like anxiety, depression, or bipolar disorder.

Also, there's still a lingering belief that ADHD is primarily a "boy" condition. This bias can influence how doctors and even parents perceive symptoms in girls and women. Historically, ADHD research has focused more on males, leaving gaps in our understanding of ADHD in women. Many healthcare providers aren't adequately trained to recognize ADHD symptoms in women.

The result? Delayed diagnosis, frustration, and missed opportunities for women to get the support and help they need.

The Power of Acceptance

Accepting ADHD doesn't mean giving up. Rather, it's a way to let go of self-blame and frustration. Instead of fighting against how your brain is wired, take advantage of your neurodiversity and explore it to the fullest.

Acceptance also helps you understand your thoughts and feelings more clearly. This way, you can find ways to deal with the real issue, identify your personal values, and live a life that is aligned with these values. It's particularly effective because you focus on accepting, rather than trying to change or control, your thoughts and feelings.

Mindfulness is encompassed in acceptance, and it involves being present in the moment without judgment. This helps you reduce the power of unhelpful thoughts and makes you more aware of your choices. (Imagine moving straight past the buzzing bees so you can reach for the honey.)

Acceptance also helps you reduce emotional stress and tension. When you *radically accept*, you get to reduce that torturous emotional turmoil and find peace. You also get to be more flexible—that is, you develop mental flexibility. This allows you to adapt to situations and find new ways to approach issues. Actually, when you accept your distractions and refocus your attention, you increase your ability to concentrate. And that's a good thing.

I'm not asking you to give up or ignore your problems; all I'm saying is you have the power to choose how to respond to issues in a way that aligns with your values and goals. And you can do that by accepting, rather than fighting, who and what you are. Can you accept *you* for who *you* are?

ADHD and Your Identity

Last summer, I spent so much time outside just soaking up the sun's warmth. To protect my eyes from the sun, I religiously wore my sunglasses, and soon enough, it became a habit. One afternoon, as I strolled through the park, I noticed the sky darkening; it looked like it was about to rain. I hastily looked for a place to take shelter so I wouldn't get drenched.

As I looked around, I took off my sunglasses for safekeeping and almost in an instant, the cloudy skies became quite clear. It wasn't going to rain at all—it was just the effect of my sunglasses.

ADHD can significantly impact how you see yourself. It's like wearing tinted glasses that color your perceptions and experiences. It can make you feel like you don't fit in. You see the world differently, process information at a different pace, or have a unique way of approaching things. And let's not even get started on the struggles with focus, organization, or impulsivity that can lead to repeated failures or mistakes. Over time, this can erode your self-confidence and make you question your abilities.

On the flip side, ADHD can make you focused on what really interests you. This can create a strong sense of identity around these passions, making them a core part of who you are. Who knows—you could turn out to be the 21st century Mozart. You know something else I find quite interesting? Women with ADHD think outside the box and find creative solutions to problems. And who says you can't turn your impulsivity into an advantage?

A lot of women with ADHD end up becoming really good at putting on a mask. It's like you're constantly trying to cover up everything, from a tiny pimple to the deep feelings you're struggling with. We want to seem perfect, so we hide the parts of ourselves that feel messy or different. But pretending to be someone you're not is exhausting. It can make you feel fake and lonely, like there's a huge gap between who you are inside and the person you show to the world.

One way to discover your true self—beyond the diagnosis—is to ask, "What truly matters to me?" Being able to identify your core values can help you align your actions with your beliefs, providing a strong foundation for your identity. Think about what you stand for, what you believe in, and what kind of impact you want to make on the world.

Self-discovery is a lifelong journey. It's okay to take your time and explore different paths. The most important thing is to be patient with yourself and enjoy the process.

Navigating Diagnosis

Upon diagnosis, it's okay to feel a mix of emotions. Give yourself time to absorb the news and process it in its entirety. Next, gather as many resources as you need. Learn as much as you can about ADHD. Understanding the condition will help you manage it better. As you give yourself time, you need to also give yourself some grace as you figure things out. Break down big goals into smaller, manageable steps to avoid feeling overwhelmed and stay motivated.

Get enough sleep and stay active. This is no time to withdraw; rather, it is time to radically accept and work out strategies that will help you thrive. These daily habits will really help you feel better overall. Everyone's different, so try out different approaches to see what works best for you.

And remember to give yourself a pat on the back as you make progress. Even small progress is worth acknowledging—it keeps you moving forward and boosts your confidence. You are likely to get stressed either physically or mentally upon receiving your diagnosis. Find things that can help you unwind. You could play games, watch movies, read books, or even take more time to sleep. Do things you love doing. Find what brings you peace.

Worksheet: Personal ADHD Discovery Journal

Which of these traits resonate most with you? Check all that apply:

- Difficulty paying attention to details ✓
- Trouble staying focused on tasks ✓
- Frequent forgetfulness ✓
- Fidgeting or squirming ✓
- Difficulty waiting turns ✓
- Interrupting others ✓
- Trouble organizing tasks ✓
- Avoiding mentally demanding tasks ✓
- Losing things easily ✓
- Distractibility ✓

Describe other ADHD traits you notice.

_____

_____

_____

_____

_____

What was your initial reaction to your diagnosis? How do you feel?

_____

_____

_____

_____

_____

How has ADHD affected your life? Write out some impacts and challenges you've faced.

Area of Life	Specific Impact of ADHD	Challenges Faced
Work/School		
Relationships		
Hobbies/Interests		
Daily Routines		
Self-esteem		
Other:		

CHAPTER TWO

Core Concepts of Dialectical Behavior Therapy (DBT)

❧

"He who controls others may be powerful, but he who has mastered himself is mightier still."

—Lao Tzu

"He who is slow to anger is better than the mighty, And he who rules his spirit than he who takes a city."

—Proverbs 16:32 (NKJV)

Case Study

I didn't particularly enjoy high school. It was a minefield, maybe not literally but it was close to it. My brain felt like a pinball machine on overdrive—constantly bouncing off thoughts, emotions, and everything in between. It got so bad that even talking to my mom felt like walking on eggshells. One minute I was fine, the next I'd be a sobbing mess over something totally insignificant.

Therapy helped a little, but it felt like talking in circles. Then, my therapist suggested something called DBT. It sounded weird—"dialectical" what? But hey, I was desperate. And goodness me, it worked! I began to see ADHD for what it was: a noisy roommate, not the boss of my life. My relationship

with my mom improved too. We even started joking about "using my skills"
during arguments. I'm not perfect, but I'm way more confident and way
less likely to turn a bad grade into a full-blown meltdown.

Introduction to Dialectical Behavioral Therapy (DBT)

Feeling like your ADHD makes you do "too much" emotionally? Dialectical behavior therapy (DBT) can help. It's a type of therapy that teaches you skills to handle your emotions in a healthy way. I've dedicated this whole chapter to showing you how DBT can help you manage your emotions and your ADHD as a whole. Let's get started.

DBT is a modified form of cognitive behavioral therapy (CBT), and it focuses on helping you manage your emotions, cope with stress, and improve your relationships. It was developed by Dr. Marsha Linehan in the late 1980s. Initially, DBT was created to treat borderline personality disorder (BPD), but because of its effectiveness, DBT has been adapted for various other mental health conditions, including anxiety, depression, eating disorders, post-traumatic stress disorder (PTSD), and of course, ADHD.

DBT emphasizes four key skill areas. I'll give you a brief overview now, and then we'll go into more detail. The first of these key skill areas is *mindfulness*. It's easy to go through the whole day without being present in the moment. You get so lost in your thoughts and activities, it seems like you're on autopilot. Mindfulness makes you more conscious of yourself and what is going on around you. That way, you can get a grip on your thoughts, words, actions, and ultimately your life.

The second key skill is *distress tolerance*. Life isn't always going to hand you roses and violets; sometimes you have to deal with thorns and thistles. So, how do you react when unpleasant situations show up? Do you overreact or totally ignore the issue and wish it away? Distress tolerance offers techniques and tips that are beneficial even in the most awful situations.

Next up is *interpersonal effectiveness*. You don't have to shy away from new relationships just because you don't know how to handle them. Or maybe you are at a loss when it comes to handling the precious relationships around you. DBT teaches assertiveness in relationships, allowing you to express your needs while maintaining positive interactions. So, yes, you can have a great relationship with your spouse, kids, parents, and even co-workers.

Last is *emotional regulation*. We all need a dose of that every now and again, right? This skill helps you identify and modify your emotional responses. You may not be able to control other people's actions (or inaction), but you can control how these affect you and your emotions. When you recognize how you feel and intentionally choose an opposite action (even when it is not pleasant), you can learn to handle your emotions even better.

DBT Skills: Emotional Regulation

Your emotions are a very important part of your mental health. They're like your soul's nerve endings, helping you to react and respond to situations correctly. You have both positive and negative emotions, and you need to find a way to stay in balance, lest you tip over. Emotional regulation involves recognizing, understanding, and modulating your emotions to respond to these situations in a constructive manner, especially when faced with stressors or challenging situations.

Let's go on to some of these skills. I'll start with the STOP skill.

One of the foundational techniques for emotional regulation in DBT is STOP. The concept of STOP is to pause and gain control over your emotional reactions. STOP is an acronym:

Stop: When you notice that your emotions are taking control, the first step is to simply stop. You need to freeze and avoid immediate reactions. This pause prevents impulsive actions driven by intense feelings. You can also name the emotions so you can clarify what you're experiencing.

Take a Step Back: Give yourself some distance from the situation. Take a deep breath and allow yourself the time to calm down. This keeps you from making rash decisions based on fleeting emotions.

Observe: Pay attention to your surroundings and your internal state. Identify the thoughts and feelings that come up, including any automatic negative thoughts (ANTs). ANTs are thoughts that come up unproved, some arising from outdated beliefs formed in childhood. When you truly observe, you can gather important information about the situation and your emotional responses.

Proceed Carefully: Once you've taken time to reflect, ask yourself guiding questions like, "What do I want from this situation?" or "What choice could improve things?" This helps you be more conscious and deliberate about how to respond.

Another emotional regulation technique that I have found to be really effective is the Opposite Action Skill. Let me break it down. Emotions are biologically wired to elicit specific responses—for instance, when you are angry, you want to attack; when you are afraid, the instinctive response is to cower. What the Opposite Action Skill helps you do is to counteract these instinctive reactions. Let me give you some examples.

Instead of acting aggressively when you are angry, you can choose to be calm, be kind, or simply walk away if you cannot bear the situation. Rather than isolating yourself because you feel ashamed, you can choose to hold your head high and push yourself to interact with others. Instead of avoiding a situation, confront it and build your courage. When feeling inactive, push yourself to take action. Instead of rejecting or avoiding, work through the situation. Instead of hiding when you feel guilty, take responsibility and apologize sincerely.

Interpersonal Effectiveness

Interpersonal effectiveness, in layman's terms, is basically the art of adulting your social interactions. It involves working through the messy world of human connections with a little more grace and a lot less drama. Misunderstandings and miscommunications can fuel workplace drama faster than you can say "office gossip." But you can learn to master your relationships and avoid these pitfalls. You'll learn to express yourself clearly and listen actively.

Life is more fun with strong connections. Interpersonal effectiveness gives you all you need to build strong bonds and cultivate already-existing relationships. You'll become a better listener, a more empathetic friend, and someone people enjoy spending time with.

Interpersonal effectiveness is not an innate ability. You need to learn and practice, but it pays off in the long run. The goal of interpersonal effectiveness is to help you meet your needs by correctly communicating those needs and desires to others. You'll also gain respect and ensure that your opinions and feelings are taken seriously. As they should be. There are four skills for interpersonal effectiveness, and I will discuss each of them, starting with the acronym DEAR MAN.

DEAR MAN helps in effective communication. It helps you give a clear and articulate voice to how you feel. Let me explain what each letter stands for.

Describe: Clearly describe the current situation, sticking to the facts without mixing things up. State exactly what prompted your feelings.

Express: Share your feelings and opinions directly. Don't assume the other person knows how you feel. Be as clear as possible.

Assert: Make your request or say "No" with confidence. Be explicit about what you want or don't want.

Reinforce: Explain the positive outcomes of meeting your needs, as well as the potential negative consequences of not doing so.

Mindful: Stay focused on your goals throughout the conversation. If distractions or attacks occur, maintain your position and reiterate your message.

Appear Confident: Use a steady tone of voice, maintain eye contact, and exhibit open body language to convey confidence.

Negotiate: Be open to compromise. Consider alternative solutions that satisfy both parties.

Another interpersonal effectiveness skill is GIVE. Yeah, it's another acronym. One of the things I absolutely love about DBT is the use of acronyms you can easily remember. It sprinkles a little fun into this tough work. Just like DEAR MAN, GIVE also helps in effective communication, but it takes a little different approach. Let's get on with it:

(be) **G**entle: Approach discussions respectfully. Avoid aggressive language, threats, or manipulation. Express your feelings calmly, without exaggeration.

(act) **I**nterested: Show genuine interest in the other person's perspective. Listen actively and patiently.

Validate: Acknowledge the other person's feelings and viewpoints. Showing that you understand and care about the other party's feelings helps you both connect better.

(use an) **E**asy manner: Maintain a lighthearted tone. Use humor when appropriate to ease tension.

Let me highlight one last skill before going further. This is the FAST skill. It's one thing to get your thoughts across; it's another to get them across without losing your self-respect. Let me show you how.

(be) **F**air: Ensure that you consider both your needs and the other person's feelings.

(no) **A**pologies: Avoid excessive apologies. Don't apologize for your existence or for having an opinion.

Stick to Your Values: Stick with your core values and beliefs without compromising them for trivial reasons.

(be) **T**ruthful: No beating around the bush. Avoid exaggeration or deceit, and present your feelings honestly.

The topic of interpersonal effectiveness wouldn't be complete without talking about boundaries. Growing up in a chaotic environment can make it difficult to recognize and establish personal boundaries. But you need to understand and enforce your boundaries so you can be emotionally healthy.

To set effective boundaries, you need to know what is non-negotiable for you. This can include physical boundaries (your comfort with personal space and physical interactions) and emotional boundaries (protecting yourself from emotional harm, such as ridicule or manipulation). Once you've identified your boundaries, communicate them clearly. You can make use of any of the skills I shared earlier. Trust me, it will help.

Distress Tolerance: Navigating Life's Challenges with Resilience

So, how do you respond when life gives you thorns instead of roses? Distress tolerance, as we mentioned at the start of this chapter, is a skill that helps you to cope with difficult emotions and situations. It emphasizes the importance of learning to endure pain and distress skillfully. By developing distress tolerance skills, you can manage your reactions to distressing situations, helping you get through crises without resorting to impulsive or harmful behaviors.

At the very core of distress tolerance is acceptance: the ability to perceive reality as it is, without trying to change it. You can't always avoid pain, but when you learn to accept and work through it, you can improve the outcome of the situation. This gives you a balanced mindset and perspective.

Distress tolerance can be easily incorporated into your daily life. For example, ACCEPTS is a structured approach that helps you cope with distress through distraction. Might sound a little out of place, but trust me, it's effective. Let me break down the acronym:

Activities: Participate in activities that occupy your mind and body. Watch a movie, clean, exercise, or spend time with your friends. When you stay active, you can easily divert your attention from the distressing situation.

Contributions: Shift focus by helping others. Sometimes, we find ease and comfort when we bring ease and comfort to others. Volunteer work or simple acts of kindness can give you the needed sense of purpose and connection.

Comparisons: Sometimes, comparisons can help. See how your current feelings compare to past experiences. As you do so, you'll see that you've been able to pull through worse scenarios. And if what you're currently facing is the worst so far, reflecting on how you've been able to navigate previous tough situations will help you get through this current situation.

Emotions: Expose yourself to different emotions through music, movies, or books. Experiencing a range of emotions can help you break the cycle of negative feelings.

Pushing Away: Temporarily set aside the distressing situation. You can visualize pushing it away or boxing it up to deal with later.

Thoughts: Engage your mind in counting or puzzles to distract yourself from painful emotions.

Sensations: Use physical sensations to ground yourself. Squeeze a stress ball, take a hot shower, or hold ice in your hand to shift your focus.

Another skill I'd like to share with you is TIP. It helps you to quickly alter your body chemistry to disband overwhelming emotions. Here is what it means to TIP:

Tip the Temperature: You can splash cold water over your face to cool down. A temperature change is bound to induce a calming effect. This can involve holding ice or submerging your face in cold water.

Intense Exercise: Engage in vigorous physical activity to release pent-up energy and shift your emotional state.

Paced Breathing: Slow your breathing down to regain control over your emotional responses. Focus on deep, rhythmic breaths to promote calmness.

One last skill before I move on. Ever been caught in a case of "should I or should I not?" Then you should try out the pros/cons approach. This is a decision-making tool that helps you weigh the benefits and drawbacks of your actions. It's particularly useful when you are faced with the urge to do something you may later regret. You can apply the pros/cons skill by first describing the dilemma you're facing; then consider both short-term and long-term effects. Analyze the advantages and disadvantages of other options available to you. If you are ever faced again with similar urges, you can check your pros and cons list. What were the positive outcomes of resisting the urge and the negative consequences of giving in? Remembering your past experiences can reinforce your resolve.

The Importance of Validation in DBT and ADHD Management

I mentioned earlier that throughout history, women have often been valued for their appearance and adherence to societal norms. Women have been taught and seen to be prim and proper. This creates a subconscious pressure for women to seek approval in order to feel worthy. We all tend to focus on information that confirms our existing beliefs. If a woman feels insecure, she looks for validation more readily and pays less attention to positive experiences that don't necessarily involve external validation.

In DBT, validation serves several key purposes. Validation enhances your emotional regulation. It helps you see that your feelings are acceptable and understandable. This way, you are able to better manage your overwhelming emotions without resorting to impulsive behaviors. Remember we talked about acceptance earlier? Learning to validate your own experiences helps you better accept yourself, leading to personal growth and emotional healing.

ADHD comes with constantly being misunderstood regarding your behaviors and struggles. Validating your experiences helps you feel seen and understood, reducing feelings of shame and frustration.

Applying DBT Skills in Daily Life

Okay, so how do you apply all these skills in your day-to-day activities? Let me run you through some scenarios and how you can apply these DBT skills. Say, for example, your kids don't listen when you ask them to clean up. You ask three more times and they ignore you. The urge is to scream, yell, and maybe use the wrong words, right? Rather than following through with that, which DBT skills would you apply?

Let's look at another scenario. A driver pulls right in front of you and you have to swerve. You have an urge to scream and give them a piece of your mind. Instead, you use gratitude that you have a car and get to drive. You smile and think of all the ways you have been blessed. That's applying the opposite action, right?

You see, integrating DBT skills into your daily life can enhance your emotional resilience, interpersonal effectiveness, and everything about you. When you use these skills regularly, you can better get through whatever comes your way and improve your overall well-being.

DBT Worksheets

Think of a recent situation that triggered you. Can you describe what happened?

_____

_____

_____

_____

_____

On a scale of 1 (barely a ripple) to 10 (full-blown emotional volcano), rate the intensity of your emotion at its peak. Mark your spot on the meter.

- 0-1
- 1-2
- 2-3
- 3-4
- 4-5
- 5-6
- 6-7

- 7-8
- 8-9
- 9-10

Did you notice the physical signs of your emotion taking hold? Did your heart rate increase? Did your muscles clench tighter? Note any physical sensations below:

- Racing Heartbeat: [Yes/No]
- Tight Muscles: [Yes/No]
- Sweating: [Yes/No]
- Shortness of Breath: [Yes/No]
- Add any other signals you noticed:
- _____
- _____
- _____

Sometimes, emotional storms require alternative routes. Check off 3 healthy coping skills you could use:

- Deep Breathing Exercises
- Progressive Muscle Relaxation
- Listening to Calming Music

Acknowledge your emotions. They are real and deserve to be heard! Write down a validating statement for yourself, like "It's okay to feel frustrated" or "This situation is upsetting, and that's valid."

- **Validation Statement**

_____

_____

_____

_____

_____

Takeaways

- Dialectical behavior therapy (DBT) is a modified form of cognitive behavioral therapy (CBT) and it focuses on helping you manage your emotions, cope with stress, and improve your relationships.

- Your emotions are a very important part of your mental health. They're like your soul's nerve endings, helping you to react and respond to situations correctly. You have both positive and negative emotions, and you need to find a way to stay in balance, lest you tip over.

- Research shows that DBT is effective for various mental health conditions beyond ADHD. It helps with borderline personality disorder, bipolar disorder, eating disorders, generalized anxiety disorder, major depressive disorder, non-suicidal self-injury, obsessive-compulsive disorder (OCD), and substance use disorders.

CHAPTER THREE

Enhancing Executive Functioning

"If someone has attention deficit hyperactivity disorder (ADHD), they have executive dysfunction. However, if someone has executive dysfunction, that doesn't mean they have ADHD."

—Billy Roberts

"Trust in the Lord with all your heart, And lean not on your own understanding; In all your ways acknowledge Him, And He shall direct your paths."

—Proverbs 3:5-6 (NKJV)

Case Study

It was in my first year of college that I was diagnosed with ADHD. This came as a total shock and disbelief to me. I have always seen myself as hardworking and intelligent, especially being a law student. It was so difficult for me to accept that I underwent several assessments, yet the result remained the same.

It was during this period my coursework became more rigorous, with exams fast approaching. As the exams drew near, my fear grew. I could not focus for extended periods and found myself easily distracted.

The thought of failure kept clouding my mind. I realized with exams a few months away that if I didn't find a solution to this distraction, my future career prospects would be in jeopardy.

My counselor introduced me to a therapist who helped me manage my distractions and ADHD. I finally understood why I had been distracted and was able to connect my experiences to my ADHD. I decided to learn more about ADHD and seek strategies to help me manage my distractions.

I joined a community of people like me and learned from their experiences. I tried to explore coping mechanisms and used different technological tools to help me navigate my exams and manage distractions.

I was overwhelmed and joyous when I received my spring semester result. It was far better than the fall, and this made me see my ADHD as a strength. As I learned that many successful professionals have ADHD, I was inspired to do more.

Throughout my college experience, I was one of the top three students, even as an ADHD woman.

—Ashley

Why Executive Functioning Matters

Executive functioning (EF) involves many skills that are needed in breaking down big tasks into smaller, manageable steps, setting realistic deadlines, and deciding what needs to be done first. It also helps you keep track of your belongings, schedules, and information, estimate how long tasks will take, and stay focused even when there are distractions. You may ask, why are EF skills so important? Simply put, EF helps you put your life (work, marriage, school, and everything else) in order.

Say, for example, you are working on a research project; EF helps you settle on a topic, organize your findings, and manage your time so you finish before the deadline. But if your EF isn't strong, you will keep going around in circles, finding it hard to focus on even the simplest tasks.

EF includes several key parts, and each has a role to play in how you think and feel. The first EF skill I will be addressing is *metacognition*. This means "thinking about thinking." It helps you figure out what you already know and what you still need to learn so you can choose the best way to learn it. In simpler terms, metacognition helps you to be more conscious of your thoughts so you are fully aware of what you know, what you don't know, what you have done, and what needs to be done.

There is also *impulse control*, which helps you stop and think before you act. It helps you avoid saying things too quickly, rushing through your work, or making risky choices.

Emotional control is about managing your feelings in a way that helps you deal with problems and keep your focus on your goals.

Flexibility is being able to change your plans and come up with new ideas when things don't go the way you expected.

There is also *working memory*, which is like a temporary storage area in your brain where you can hold information while you're using it to do something. It's really important for following instructions and doing things that have lots of steps.

The good news is that you can get better at EF skills with time and practice. Getting better at your EF skills is setting yourself up for success in all ways.

Understanding Executive Dysfunction in ADHD Women

Executive dysfunction occurs when there are challenges with your EF skills, making it difficult to pay attention, manage time, or break down big tasks. Executive dysfunction is common in individuals with ADHD due to a difference in their brain function, especially in the basal ganglia and prefrontal cortex, which are mostly responsible for EF skills.

Executive dysfunction symptoms can vary by individual. Symptoms may include difficulty in retaining small details, difficulty in setting goals, lack of concentration, difficulty in solving problems, difficulty in organizing, and lack of time management. People exhibit all or some of the symptoms.

Women with ADHD may face additional challenges with executive dysfunction, as they have to juggle multiple roles, and balancing these roles might be difficult.

Prioritization and Time Management: DBT Approaches

Poor time management can have a serious influence on your relationships, finances, work, health, school, personal life, and self-confidence. Improving your time management skills can help improve your overall quality of life. DBT has been proven to be effective in improving EF skills, as it focuses more on practical skills and managing emotions. There are several DBT approaches you can use in prioritization and time management. Let's get into it.

There are 3 major ways you can approach thoughts running through your mind: with an emotional mind (feeling overwhelmed), a rational mind (acting logically without considering the emotional impact), or a wise mind. The **wise mind** is the balance between the emotional mind and rational mind. This implies that you use your heart and your brain to make decisions. For instance, say you need to finish a project and you also want to catch up with the latest gossip on Instagram. Your emotional mind will feel like spending all day going from one Reel to another while your rational mind will encourage you to work and not take a break. The wise mind will help you find a balance and prioritize the tasks effectively.

Intense emotions can lead to unhealthy coping mechanisms, which can greatly affect time management and lead to procrastination. **Emotional regulation** techniques can help you manage your emotions better. You can also use the **DEAR MAN** technique we discussed in the previous chapter to set boundaries and say no to additional tasks. **TIP** can help you to stay calm when you feel panicked about meeting a deadline. (Revisit Chapter Two to remind yourself of the details of applying these approaches.)

DBT skills should be incorporated into your daily activities, as they require consistency and practice.

Task Initiation and Follow-Through Strategies

I decided I was going to read a book during my vacation for self-improvement. I could feel the excitement rushing through me as I read a few pages of the book, but the excitement didn't last long, and I stopped reading midway. Was the book not interesting? Believe me when I say the book had all it takes to keep me glued to my seat, but the problem was with *follow-through*.

Task initiation means getting started on something. Some may find it difficult to start something, but it's equally important to be able to follow through with it. In the words of writer and public speaker Robin Sharma: *"Starting strong is good. Finishing strong is epic."*

There are several factors that can be an obstacle to task initiation and following through. Complex tasks can lead to avoidance, procrastination, or distraction. If you are a perfectionist, you might not start or complete a task due to fear of making mistakes. Working memory deficit can also make it hard to keep track of steps. Or perhaps you start the tasks you want to do, but fail to follow through to the end. So, how do you go about this?

Start small. When you feel a task is overwhelming or too large to complete, break it down into manageable mini-tasks. You can use the **Pomodoro technique**, which involves working for a set period followed by a short break. If you have to do a less pleasant task, you can try to combine it with a task you enjoy. Reframe negative patterns. Set goals that are achievable and can be completed within the duration of time you assigned. You can have someone check in on you to provide motivation.

What about ensuring that you follow through? Set deadlines and establish a routine that will help you to be consistent with it. Do the important tasks first and reward yourself after the completion of each task. You can also take breaks. There's nothing stopping you from taking a power nap when you need to—but don't forget to set your alarm!

Managing Distractions and Maintaining Focus

Distraction has become a common challenge that affects our productivity and task execution. With the constant notifications from our smartphone, focusing has become so hard to do. Distraction can be either internal or external. Internal distractions are caused by our thoughts or emotions while external distractions are caused by the environment. Whichever one you are affected by, distractions are bound to take your time and attention. Though avoiding distraction might seem impossible, you can manage it. You just need precise strategies and a lot of commitment.

To start with, you need to understand the nature of your distraction. Are you faced with an external or internal one? This will help you in creating a distraction-free environment. Organize your tasks the day before and write them in order of importance (ensure you incorporate regular breaks or physical activity in between to avoid burnout). And while your smartphone can be a hub of distraction, you can also use it to keep you focused. Use productivity tools or apps that block distractions and turn off notifications during work hours. Sometimes stress can influence distraction, so find a way to calm your body to reduce stress. (You can find more tips for eliminating distractions in Chapter Six.)

I guess you've probably heard of **SMART goals** (Specific, Measurable, Achievable, Realistic and Time-bound). Let me use a workplace example. Instead of the goal "get a promotion," define what success looks like. Maybe it's "deliver a presentation on [topic] to senior management by [date]." Don't leave your goals to chance. Be specific. Track your progress. Did you complete a training course relevant to the promotion?

Schedule regular check-ins with your manager to discuss your career development. That makes your goal measurable.

Be ambitious but realistic. Consider your workload and responsibilities. Can you break down the promotion goal into smaller, achievable steps like taking on a project or leading a team? It's easy to achieve your goals that way.

How relevant is your goal? Is this promotion aligned with your long-term career goals? Maybe it opens doors to a specific area of interest or leadership opportunities. Ensure your goal fuels your overall career aspirations. Do you really need this promotion for your long-term goal, or would you rather divert that strength to something else?

Don't let your goals float indefinitely. Set a target date for your presentation, training completion, or when you'll have a conversation with your manager. Don't give in to procrastination, either. Have a goal? Make it SMART. Do it now.

Building and Sustaining Organizational Habits

Your thoughts become your words, your words become your actions, and your repeated actions become a habit. Habits play an important role in shaping our behavior and smashing our goals. Our habits frequently put us in a loop of daily activities that we complete without necessarily making the decision to do so. Habits form around 40% of our behavior and can actually help us change things we have been struggling with, including being organized.

Organizational habits involve a regular routine of keeping things structured and easy to work through. Disorderliness can keep you from reaching your goals and being productive. ADHD makes it even more difficult. Remember we talked about working memory? That also comes into play here. A deficit in working memory leads to difficulty staying organized. Lack of organizational habits can lead to procrastination, inability to break down tasks, and difficulty with follow-through.

Before I go on to building organizational skills, I'll give you a quick rundown on how habits work. Habits follow four key stages: cue, cravings, response, and reward. Cue is the trigger, cravings is the desire to do it, response is the action you take because of the cravings, and reward is the satisfaction you derive from it. These four concepts determine how habits stick. The question is, how do we build organizational habits?

Start small to avoid feeling overwhelmed. Set an external reminder as a cue to help you remember multiple details and take action immediately. Setting a time limit for each task can make the task more enjoyable and keep you motivated. You can use visual tools like a calendar or checklist to help you keep track of your tasks and deadlines, but ensure your checklist is brief so as to achieve everything on it.

Reward yourself each time you finish a task. You can add new habits to your existing ones to make them easier to adopt.

Examples of organizational habits to start with include assigning a designated place for different items and throwing away unneeded items. Even something as small as simplifying your wardrobe or switching to online banking rather than paper can help.

Share your goals with your friends. Building and sustaining organizational habits is possible with commitment and patience. Be compassionate and patient with yourself when setbacks occur.

Memory Enhancement Tips

Working memory is also known as short-term memory and refers to the ability to hold information temporarily so that it is accessible when you need to act on it. This is essential for tasks like making decisions or solving problems. For instance, say you are out shopping for groceries or trying to decide what to wear. Your working memory will help you to remember what you need to buy or recall any important events that day to help you choose the best outfit. Memory problems can affect your daily activities, relationships, and work. Whatever you need to do, you need your working memory to accomplish it.

Fortunately, you can enhance your memory by following these practical tips. The first step is to understand how your memory works and accept your working memory deficit. Break down big chunks of information into smaller pieces; focus on and complete one task before moving to the next to avoid distraction. You can organize the information into categories to help you remember easily.

You can incorporate visual aids like images or symbols to help you retain more information. Set alarms and reminders for important duties and take note of every bit of information. You can also use a to-do list to list out your daily activities and tick them off when done.

I love using mnemonics. I picked this up while studying for exams in high school, and that habit has stuck over the years. Mnemonics and rhymes help you recall information. Use acronyms, or create songs or rhymes to help you remember things. Repeat information to yourself and review at regular intervals to reinforce memory. You can even create a story to link different pieces of information.

Talking about what you need to remember can also help. The more you talk about it and actively engage your mind, the less likely you are to forget that piece of information. Talk to someone about your activities and repeat it to yourself to reinforce your retention. In addition, take care of your physical health: exercise regularly, eat a healthy diet to boost brain function, get enough sleep, and stick to a regular routine to avoid overloading yourself.

The Role Technology Plays

Let's say you had a list of activities you wanted to do in preparation for Christmas. Juggling these activities can make you forget which are most important. What if you could incorporate technology to remind you of each activity? Your task would become easier, don't you think?

Technology is growing rapidly and has become an asset for all. It is an excellent tool for addressing problems relating to ADHD such as time management, task initiation, memory enhancement, and many others. Leveraging these tools can help you to manage symptoms and improve daily functioning. Fortunately, these tools are available at your fingertips.

To aid time management, tools like Google Calendar, Microsoft Outlook, and Todoist can help set reminders, manage your schedule and task list, and help break down tasks. These applications also have features like notifications and setting up recurring events.

For managing distractions, you can make use of features on your phone like focus mode. Apps like Focus Booster can help you block distraction and avoid burnout. You can also use extensions like StayFocused to block distracting websites.

Apps like OneNote can help you organize information in one place. Mind mapping tools like Coggle and Xmind can help you visualize your ideas. You can even make use of mood tracking apps like Moodfit and Moodpath to help you track your mood over time and identify recurring patterns.

You can join online communities such as on Facebook, Reddit, or online forums to share your experience, get advice, and relate to other neurodivergent women. Websites can help you stay updated and get resources with the latest information on ADHD. Through technology, it is possible to enhance your quality of life, boost confidence, and manage your ADHD effectively.

Worksheet: Weekly Planning and Reflection

List 5 goals you plan to achieve for the week in order of priority.

    1. _____

    2. _____

    3. _____

    4. _____

    5. _____

Fill in your daily to-do list:

Monday

    1. _____

    2. _____

    3. _____

Tuesday

1. _____

2. _____

3. _____

Wednesday

1. _____

2. _____

3. _____

Thursday

1. _____

2. _____

3. _____

Friday

1. _____

2. _____

3. _____

Saturday

1. _____

2. _____

3. _____

Sunday

1. _____

2. _____

3. _____

What tasks did you complete this week?

_____

_____

What challenges did you face while completing them?

_____

How did you manage distractions?

_____

Check all that apply to you:

- I use memory aids
- I get help to organize my time
- I leverage technology to manage my distractions
- I eat healthy food with lots of nutrients
- I use a visual planner to organize my tasks

How do you initiate and follow through on tasks?

_____

What new strategies will you try next week?

_____

How will you address any obstacles?

_____

List 5 things you did well this week:

1. _____

2. _____

3. _____

4. _____

5. _____

Takeaways

- Executive dysfunction is commonly attributed to ADHD but is more prominent and challenging for women, massively affecting their daily activities.

- With DBT therapy, challenges associated with executive dysfunction like prioritization can be controlled.

- Task initiation and follow-through can be challenging for those with ADHD.

- As technology evolves, several technological tools have been developed to help manage distractions and other executive dysfunction challenges relating to ADHD.

PART TWO

Thriving with ADHD

W ho says you have to thrive "despite" ADHD? That's a bit of an outdated mindset, isn't it? It implies that ADHD is something to overcome, rather than a unique way of experiencing the world.

Shifting the mindset from "overcoming" to "thriving" allows you to focus on personal development and achieving your goals. That way, you can recognize your strengths and accomplishments so you can boost self-esteem and confidence.

While it's true that ADHD comes with a lot of downs, it also comes with a host of ups. Creativity, energy, and a different perspective are just a few examples. So, instead of focusing on thriving "despite" ADHD, why not focus on thriving *with* it?

CHAPTER FOUR

Enhancing Emotional Intelligence

"The sign of an intelligent person is their ability to control their emotions by the application of reason."

—Marya Mannes

"He who is slow to anger is better than the mighty, And he who rules his spirit than he who takes a city."

—Proverbs 16:32 (NKJV)

Case Study

Ever since I was little, I always wanted to have my own company, having always been at the top of my class. I thought I had all it takes to find success. I am intelligent and have innovative ideas and technical skills to bring a business to success. I never knew I was missing an important piece of the puzzle. Getting potential investors and partners was hard; I couldn't communicate my ideas successfully to my investors, as I used too many technical words during my presentation.

I was running low on funds and had to take on personal debt. It was hard for me to get visibility and customers. I had to close down and stay indoors, isolating myself from family and friends. At one point I was having suicidal thoughts and could only think of ending it all.

My brother forced me to attend a leadership development program and visit a therapist. This was a turning point for me. I learned that what I was lacking was emotional intelligence. I picked up my business ideas and started all over again. Investors were happy with my ideas, as I communicated my ideas to them effectively (something I once thought was not valuable).

Within a year, my business has grown rapidly. I've been able to collaborate with other companies and hire top talent. I'm able to better manage my stress and emotions also. My business is gaining more visibility, and not only that, my relationships with my friends and family have improved—they all love to have me around.

—Evelyn

What is Emotional Intelligence?

Emotional intelligence, often called EQ, is basically your ability to understand and manage your own feelings and to understand and relate to the feelings of others. It's like having a built-in emotional GPS. It includes a range of skills you need to influence others' behavior and make informed decisions. The concept of EQ dates back to the early 1960s when it was studied by researchers Peter Salavoy and John Mayer, but it was later popularized in 1995 by Daniel Goleman.

You've probably heard that smart people are successful. Well, that's not always true! While having a high IQ (intelligence quotient) can help you ace tests and get into a good school, it's not the whole story. IQ is basically a measure of how well you can solve puzzles and think logically. It's like a score in a brain game.

But EQ is arguably even more important. Research shows that EQ is actually more impactful than IQ when it comes to success in life and work. People with high EQ tend to be happier, healthier, and better at handling life's ups and downs. So, while a high IQ can open some doors, it's your EQ that will help you walk through them and make the most of the opportunities inside.

This whole EQ thing is broken down into five main parts, according to Daniel Goleman. It starts with *self-awareness*—knowing yourself really well, understanding your own feelings, strengths, and weaknesses, and how they affect others. It includes, for example, knowing when you're feeling grumpy and why, or recognizing that you're really good at problem-solving.

Next is *self-regulation*. This is about controlling your emotions. You are able to calm down when you're angry or excited, or bounce back quickly from setbacks. You have a grip on your emotions and you do not let your feelings run the show.

The next is *motivation*, which is about being driven and passionate. Motivation is what makes you go a step further even when you don't feel like it. It's that inner push that keeps you going, even when things get tough.

Second to last is *empathy*. Empathy helps you understand the feelings of others—the ability to put yourself in someone else's shoes and see things from their point of view. That way, you are able to care about what others are going through.

Last is *social skills*. With good social skills, you can interact with others smoothly, communicate effectively, build relationships, and work well in a team. Have you heard the term "people person"? That's what social skills help you do.

So, in a nutshell, EQ helps you become emotionally smart and savvy. You know yourself, manage your feelings, understand others, and build strong relationships. The level of these components determine the level of your EQ. Why is EQ important in day to day life?

Clear communication does not necessarily mean effective communication. When your emotions are not in check, you are unlikely to get the desired results. Effective communication contributes to successful teamwork, leadership, and collaboration, and this will help you a lot in your chosen career and in life. Humans have emotions that can't be dealt with through logic. EQ helps us to deal with conflicts and social complexities constructively and to maintain healthy relationships.

Uncontrolled stress can make you vulnerable to anxiety and cause health problems. EQ helps you to manage stress and mental health problems. It will make your emotions work for you and not against you. It is a vital skill set that can give you a more balanced, fulfilling, and successful life.

The Connection Between ADHD and Emotional Intelligence

I am a fan of soccer games and love seeing how each game unfolds. What fascinates me is how the coach motivates the players to keep up with the constantly moving ball throughout the match. This is similar to how EQ works with ADHD; it serves as a coach or a guide that helps you work through the challenges that ADHD brings, including inattention and lack of self-awareness.

Although EQ is important in dealing with ADHD, mastering EQ isn't so easy. Why?

ADHD makes it hard to understand your emotions, and this leads to frequent emotional outbursts. I see this more often in people who are not self-aware and, thus, have low EQ. ADHD women also find it hard to manage stress and maintain their relationships, which in turn can cause difficulty in regulating their emotions.

There is also a barrage of constant criticism from the outside world, which can affect social skills. This makes it hard for those with ADHD to communicate effectively, have productive social interactions, and respond to emotional cues.

Now, the components that create the foundation for strong emotional intelligence are not easy to come by. The good news is they can be learned. You can build your emotional intelligence. Just because it's hard, doesn't mean it's impossible to develop. It is a skill that can be learned and grown.

Emotional Awareness: Recognizing ADHD Triggers

I mentioned something about emotional awareness earlier. Let me go a little deeper. Emotional awareness is a big component of EQ; it is the ability to recognize your own emotions and those of others. Living with ADHD means you are constantly faced with managing your emotions. In emotional awareness, you understand your emotions better so when things get rough, you are able to handle it well.

Emotional awareness can help you communicate your emotions clearly to others and understand them better. Being emotionally aware gives you access to more joy and fulfillment. Understanding your emotions will help you to take care of yourself and learn from yourself. Not only that, it will improve symptoms of anxiety, addiction, depression, eating disorders, and other health problems.

Emotional awareness occurs on five levels, called the Level of Emotional Awareness Scale (LEAS) as proposed by Lane et al. (1990). It explains how emotions progress from basic recognition to complex integration.

Physical sensation is the most basic level. You know something's up, but you can't quite put your finger on it. It's like your body is trying to tell you something, but it's speaking in code. For example, you might feel a knot in your stomach or a racing heart, but you're not sure why. You're basically just reacting to physical sensations.

The second is the *emotional label.* You can now put a name to your feelings. You might say, "I'm angry" or "I'm feeling sad," but you're not entirely sure why you're feeling this way. It's like recognizing a friend from afar but not knowing their full story.

The next is *emotional expression.* Not only can you identify your feelings, but you can also express them to others. You can say, "I'm feeling frustrated because…" and explain what's bothering you. It's like having a conversation with yourself and being able to share your thoughts with someone else.

Emotional understanding is where things get interesting. You can now figure out why you're feeling a certain way. You can connect your emotions to specific events or situations. It's like you are a detective and you are getting a lead to solve the case about why you feel the way you do.

The final level is *complex emotion integration.* You can handle multiple emotions at once, and you know how to deal with tricky situations.

You're a pro at juggling feelings and making smart decisions. This is where you want to be.

But why is it sometimes so hard to keep your cool? Well, it all comes down to our brain. Your brain has a little alarm system called the amygdala. It's like your body's panic button. When something scary happens, the amygdala lights up, telling your body to either fight, flee, or freeze. This is a totally normal reaction, but sometimes, it can get a bit overzealous. When this happens, your rational brain takes a backseat, and your emotions take the wheel.

To better manage your emotions, it's helpful to understand what sets you off. Pay attention to your feelings throughout the day. What situations or people trigger strong emotional responses?

You can keep a journal to write down your daily experiences; this will help you pinpoint the triggers. Pay attention to the things in your environment like noise or stress that can trigger your emotional response. When you understand what stresses you, you can develop good strategies to manage it well. You can even ask those around you; they may notice emotional triggers that you are unaware of.

Emotional Dysregulation in ADHD

Let's say you've had a hectic week. You were up late every night, you're exhausted, and all you want is a good night's sleep. As you begin to drift off, suddenly, a loud noise jolts you awake. How do you react? Do you jump out of bed and yell? Or maybe you freeze in fear, heart pounding. For most people, this might be a minor annoyance, but for those with ADHD, it can trigger a much bigger emotional response.

This is where we talk about emotional dysregulation. You find it hard to control your feelings, and they can swing from one extreme to another. You might burst into tears over a small thing, or fly off the handle for no apparent reason. Why does this happen?

In people with ADHD, the amygdala can be overly sensitive, often sounding the alarm when it's not necessary. This can lead to intense emotional reactions to everyday situations. Also, people with ADHD often have an underactive prefrontal cortex (the area of the brain responsible for decision-making, problem-solving, and emotional regulation), making it harder to control impulsive reactions and manage strong emotions.

ADHD's executive function challenges can contribute to emotional dysregulation by making it harder to cope with stress and frustration. Many people with ADHD also have sensory processing issues. Overwhelming sensory input can trigger strong emotional responses.

Things like hyperactivity and impulsivity can also make it harder to manage emotions. You might be so focused on what you're doing that you don't notice how you're feeling. And if you also have other mental health conditions, like anxiety or depression, emotional dysregulation can be even more challenging.

Now to the big question: How do you regulate your emotions?

Emotional Regulation Strategies

You don't have to bottle up your emotions or even avoid them. Emotional regulation is a way of responding to your emotions in a healthy way—the ability to exert control over your emotions. It is not a static behavior and can be learned and improved.

First off, let's talk about *prevention*. Think of it like putting on a seatbelt before you start a really bumpy ride. One way to keep your emotions in check is to take care of yourself. Make sure you're eating right, getting enough sleep, and moving your body. These things might sound simple, but they're like fuel for your brain. Plus, they help you stay calm and focused.

Another thing to think about is avoiding things that can mess with your mood, like too much alcohol or drugs. These can make your emotions go haywire. One minute you're feeling great, the next, you're crashing hard. They can amplify your emotions, making you feel happier or sadder than usual. And when the effects wear off, you can be left feeling even worse.

It's like trying to balance on a tightrope while someone keeps shaking the rope. Not fun, right? That's why it's important to be mindful of how much you're consuming and to know when to say no. Your mental health is important, and sometimes, the best thing you can do is give your brain a break from these substances.

It's also important to feel good about yourself. When you believe in your abilities, you're more likely to step outside your comfort zone and try new things, as well as bounce back from failures more easily. Plus, people are naturally drawn to confidence. Indeed, believing in yourself is the first step to making your dreams a reality.

Planning for your emotions might sound strange, but it's actually a good thing. Think of it like preparing for a weather forecast. You don't control the storm, but you can prepare for it. Some situations tend to trigger strong emotions. By anticipating these situations, you can prepare your coping strategies. While you can't control your emotions entirely, planning helps you feel more in control of how you react and lessen the impact of unexpected emotional surges. When you're calm and prepared, you're more likely to make thoughtful choices. And by practicing coping strategies, you build emotional resilience over time.

Staying in the moment is also a good one. When things get overwhelming, try to focus on what's happening right now, not what might happen. This is because focusing on what *might* happen can actually make things feel worse. Focusing on the here and now helps to reduce anxiety. When you're caught up in what *might* happen, your body goes into fight-or-flight mode. Grounding yourself in the present can help calm your nervous system. Also, stepping back from the situation can help you see it more clearly and rationally. When you're not overwhelmed by emotions, you're better equipped to make thoughtful choices.

Constructive Alternatives for Maladaptive Behaviors

There are two ways to deal with your emotions: the healthy way (adaptive) and the unhealthy way (maladaptive). Maladaptive behaviors will stop you from effectively regulating your emotions. They are behaviors that prevent you from addressing your problems in constructive ways.

Maladaptive behaviors can be expressed through avoidance (that is, you avoid challenges instead of confronting them). For example, someone suffering from stage fright may resort to avoiding any opportunity to stand in front of a crowd instead of addressing the fear. Avoidance can lead to isolation and withdrawal from social interactions.

Another is passive-aggressive behavior. These behaviors are used to express your anger indirectly to the people who hurt you rather than addressing it openly. It can be expressed through sarcasm, subtle sabotage, the silent treatment, withholding information, etc. For example, your friend decides to bail out on a planned event at the last minute, without proper explanation. Rather than expressing how you feel, you say you are fine.

Maladaptive behaviors can prevent you from reaching the peak of emotional awareness; once you recognize this pattern, finding constructive alternatives can help you regulate your emotional responses.

While maladaptive behaviors can give you temporary relief, they often make underlying issues even worse. One adaptive coping mechanism you can build is to maintain strong relationships with those around you. You don't have to do it all alone. Share your feelings with your friends or family, or anyone you trust and feel safe with. You also need to take time out for self-care. Getting enough sleep and eating well helps to keep your emotions in check. You'll be cranky if you're sleep deprived or hungry.

I created a table to help you compare maladaptive coping strategies to adaptive ones.

Scenario	Maladaptive Coping Strategy	Result of Maladaptive Coping	Adaptive Coping Strategy	Result of Adaptive Coping

Work-related stress	Putting off tasks until the last minute	Increased stress and lower quality of work	Using time management tools like to-do lists and prioritizing tasks	Reduced stress, better productivity, and higher quality of work
Conflict with a friend	Ignoring the issue and avoiding the friend	Worsened relationship and ongoing tension	Having a calm, honest conversation to resolve the conflict	Improved relationship and resolution of conflict
Financial difficulties	Spending money impulsively to feel better	Increased debt and financial instability	Creating a budget and getting help from a financial advisor	Better financial stability and reduced stress
Academic pressure	Using substances like alcohol or drugs to cope	Poor academic performance and potential health issues	Getting help from tutors, forming study groups, and using effective study techniques	Improved academic performance and better health

Relationship problems	Blaming your partner for all issues	Increased conflict and potential breakup	Attending couples therapy or relationship counseling	Improved communication and stronger relationship
Low self-esteem	Engaging in negative self-talk	Decreased self-worth and motivation	Practicing self-compassion, using positive affirmations, and setting small, achievable goals	Increased self-esteem and motivation
Grief and loss	Withdrawing from social interactions	Feelings of isolation and prolonged grief	Talking with friends or family, or joining a support group	Emotional support and healthier processing of grief

Health issues	Ignoring symptoms and avoiding the doctor	Worsening health conditions	Scheduling regular check-ups and following the treatment plan prescribed by healthcare providers	Better health outcomes and early detection of issues
Feeling overwhelmed	Turning to food for comfort or neglecting meals	Weight issues and potential health problems	Taking a break and practicing emotional regulation techniques	Better stress management and overall health

Anxiety about the future	Imagining worst-case scenarios	Increased anxiety and inability to act	Focusing on what can be controlled, setting realistic goals, and breaking tasks into smaller steps	Reduced anxiety and more effective problem-solving

Building Resilience Through Compassion

Life is not always easy; sometimes we just have to get through the rough patches, and that takes resilience—the ability to bounce back. Your level of resilience will determine how well you are able to recover from difficult situations. The Latin phrase *amor fati*, which means "to love one's fate" (in other words, self-compassion) is a good one to keep in mind here.

Your level of resilience is a result of how much you love yourself and others. Compassion breaks you free from self-criticism and negative self-talk, opens you up to empathy and kindness, and helps you view every challenge as an opportunity to grow. Compassion also helps you to nurture and manage your emotions. It is the best way to have a wide "window of tolerance."

Be kind to yourself. Self-kindness is accepting that you can make mistakes. It is the opposite of self-judgment. Instead of criticizing yourself for your emotional outburst or forgetfulness or inadequacies, give yourself some grace. You may not be where you want to be yet, but you're definitely not where you used to be.

Resilience is like a muscle that gets stronger with exercise, and self-compassion is the key to building it. When you're compassionate towards yourself, you create a supportive inner environment that helps you cope.

How can you practice self-compassion? Recognize your humanity: Everyone experiences setbacks and failures. It's part of being human. Be kind to yourself. Don't strive for perfection. Focus on progress, not just results.

One more thing I would like to emphasize regarding self-compassion is the power of positive affirmations. These are positive statements that can help shift your mindset. Here are a few to get you started:

- I am enough, just as I am.
- I treat myself with kindness and understanding.
- It's okay to make mistakes; I am learning and growing.
- I deserve happiness and well-being.
- I release the need for perfection.
- I am worthy of love and compassion.
- I am grateful for my body and mind.
- I choose kindness towards myself today.

Worksheet: Emotion Regulation Diary

This worksheet is divided into two parts. The first part helps you to identify and track your emotions and coping strategies. In the second part, you'll examine your entries at the end of each week and reflect on what works well for you and how you can improve.

Part 1: Daily Emotion Tracking

Date: _____

Briefly describe the incident that triggered your emotions:

_____

List and identify all the emotions you felt at that time (e.g., anger, fear, frustration, etc.)

1. _____

2. _____

3. _____

4. _____

5. _____

6. _____

For each emotion you felt above, rate the intensity on a scale of 1 to 10:

1. Emotion 1: _____ Intensity: ____/10

2. Emotion 2: _____ Intensity: ____/10

3. Emotion 3: _____ Intensity: ____/10

4. Emotion 4: _____ Intensity: ____/10

5. Emotion 5: _____ Intensity: ____/10

Did you feel any physical sensations (e.g., sweating, heart racing, etc.)?

1. _____

2. _____

3. _____

4. _____

5. _____

Briefly describe what thoughts were running through your mind during this time.

_____

List out the emotion regulation strategies you're using to manage your emotions (e.g., exercise, meditation, etc.).

_____

How effective were the strategies in managing your emotions on a scale of 1 to 10?

_____/10

Part 2: Weekly Reflection

Identify the most common emotions you felt this week:

_____

Identify the strategies that were most effective:

_____

What challenges did you face in regulating your emotions?

_____

List two goals you plan on using next week to regulate your emotions. (Note: The goal must be SMART.)

1. _____

2. _____

Takeaways

- Emotional intelligence (EQ) is the ability to identify, understand, and manage your emotions and to influence the emotions of others positively.

- Hyperactivity, impulsivity, and inattentiveness contribute to emotional dysregulation for those with ADHD, which makes it difficult to manage emotional responses.

- Emotional regulation is not a static behavior and can be learned by following regulation strategies like mindfulness, empathy, and exercises to help you become emotionally aware.

- Maladaptive behaviors are behaviors that prevent you from addressing your problems in constructive ways.

- Compassion is an important tool necessary in building resilience and overcoming emotional dysregulation.

CHAPTER FIVE

Boosting Confidence and Self-Esteem

"What lies behind us and what lies before us are tiny matters compared to what lies within us."

—Ralph Waldo Emerson

"I can do all things through Christ who strengthens me."

—Philippians 4:13 (NKJV)

Case Study

My life has constantly felt like being on a hamster wheel. Right from the start, I found it difficult to stay focused and pay attention for more than a few minutes. I was tagged "too hyper." Many also complained that I moved a lot, but too much silence made me feel overwhelmed. I never saw this as a challenge until I started working at my dream company.

I was on edge, constantly feeling I was falling short as I found it impossible to stay focused and complete my tasks without interruption. It was difficult to meet deadlines, and meetings were a struggle; my mind would wander off if I wasn't the lead. I constantly doubted my abilities, shifting tasks and responsibilities to my fellow colleagues, and when I saw my colleagues calmly working on their tasks, my low self-esteem and insecurity kicked in.

A friend introduced to me a therapist who suggested incorporating "active breaks" into my routine. I found out that using fidgeting tools helped to increase my productivity. I now break my work up into shorter, manageable intervals and engage in physical activities to release pent-up energy. My ability to focus during work has increased greatly, and my confidence grew as I completed my tasks effectively. I have learned to embrace my energetic nature as a strength. Now I see my restlessness as a unique trait and not a hindrance to my success.

—Jenna

Self-Worth in the Context of ADHD

People—whether it's parents, friends, teachers, employers, or society at large—have expectations for how you should act and behave. Sometimes it's hard to live up to these expectations of being "cool, calm, and collected." Imagine hearing over and over again, "Focus! Try harder! Sit still! Not again! Stop fiddling! When will you learn?" This is one of the major issues "ADHD-ers" face as they are subjected to constant corrections and criticism, leading to them battling with embarrassment, rejection, and discouragement. Statistics show that 75% of people with ADHD report feeling like they're not good enough or smart enough.

Years of criticism and negative feedback can convince you that you are not enough, having a negative impact on your self-worth and confidence.

Self-worth is simply the way you perceive or value yourself as a person. It is how you see yourself for who you are and how much you love yourself. Having a low self-worth will greatly affect your relationships, career, and day-to-day activities, and if not properly addressed, it may lead to rejection and denial.

Many women with ADHD hide their symptoms, as they are expected to be nurturing and well-organized. I have an ADHD friend who is afraid of becoming a mother because she believes she will fail in that role. When you start seeing signs like fear, shame, hopelessness, guilt, avoidance, depression, or disengagement, or you keep saying things to yourself like, "I'm stupid, it's too hard, I hate my life"—this is a sign you are suffering from low self-worth. But you don't have to stay that way. You can change the narrative.

This is what this chapter is tailored towards: to help you accept yourself and build your confidence back. Instead of looking at yourself in the mirror and seeing the list of things you think you are not good at, you will see your unique strengths and embrace yourself for who and what you are.

Overcoming Imposter Syndrome

I remembered having a discussion with my friend Taylor; she couldn't believe her boss had commended her work. Despite the recognition, she struggled to accept it, saying, "I don't think I did well—it was just luck. What if my boss finds out later that I'm not good enough?"

Do you, like Taylor, feel like a fraud or like you are not good enough for the job you are paid to do? Do you live with the anxiety that everyone will find out you are not as capable as they think and question if your success is a result of luck or help from others? This can be a persistent shadow for individuals with ADHD. Imposter syndrome thrives on a cycle of self-validation and self-doubt. This can lead to physical exhaustion as you try to work extremely hard to cover up for your perceived inadequacies.

The first step in addressing imposter syndrome is to recognize it. Accept that these feelings are common among people with ADHD and acknowledge that your ADHD traits contribute to these feelings. Recognize your traits as a unique strength and not as a weakness, and remind yourself of your strengths on a regular basis; this will help you to see your contribution as valuable.

Feelings are different from facts. Stay with the facts: just because you think you are not good enough, doesn't mean it's true. The truth is you are capable of doing more than you think you can. Keep reminding yourself that it's your hard work that produces the result and that you are capable of learning. When you catch yourself thinking "I don't deserve it," reframe it to "It's my skill that made this possible." Pay attention to your inner dialogue and practice self-affirmation.

No matter how small your accomplishment, it deserves to be celebrated. Celebrating yourself is not showing off, but a way of reinforcing that your success is due to your efforts and abilities. It is simple and fun to do; you can keep track of your actions to help you fully own your success (I will explain more about this later in this chapter).

Not everyone is wired the same way. Don't measure your achievement in comparison to others; it will trap you into feeling like you don't measure up. Be intentional about who you follow or look up to, because being around the wrong people may contribute to your imposter syndrome and feeling of low worth. Focus more on growth than perfection. Accept that mistakes are part of learning—they don't mean you are falling short.

Reach out to supportive people who can assist you in fighting the feelings of imposter syndrome. Your talents are real. You are uniquely you.

Overcoming Self-Doubt

Self-doubt, often a silent saboteur, can significantly impact various aspects of your life. When you doubt yourself or your abilities, you're less likely to step outside your comfort zone. This hinders exploration of new opportunities, skills, and experiences, thereby restricting your personal growth. Uncertainty about your abilities can lead to paralysis by analysis. The fear of making wrong choices can prevent you from making decisions at all, leading to missed opportunities and stagnation.

Constant self-criticism fueled by self-doubt can also chip away at your self-worth. Over time, this can lead to a negative self-image and low self-esteem. Self-doubt can manifest as insecurity, making it difficult to build and maintain healthy relationships. Fear of rejection or inadequacy can create barriers in communication and connection with others. Not good, right?

Continually questioning your capabilities can also lead to chronic stress and anxiety and dampen your enthusiasm and motivation, making it hard to initiate and complete what you need to do. Fear of failure due to self-doubt often leads to procrastination. Tasks are put off, and deadlines missed, creating a cycle of stress and frustration.

Of course there will be times when we lack confidence in our abilities or feel uncertain about a situation. This is normal, particularly when you are faced with early experiences of constant criticism, corrections, and humiliation because of your ADHD traits. This negative feedback becomes internalized, leading to self-doubt.

It is best to work towards escaping the feelings of self-doubt and become more confident in your abilities by practicing some of the good habits I will explain below.

Practice self-compassion. Don't allow negative thoughts to get the best of you; say good things to yourself daily and be kind to yourself no matter the outcome. Celebrate each accomplishment. It's possible your self-doubt arises because of the way you are constantly being compared to others, leading to you receiving validation from others. To combat this, think for yourself, and don't constantly ask others what they think before making decisions.

Break down large tasks into smaller tasks; this will help you focus more on completing one step at a time and build a sense of accomplishment. Share your struggles and successes with your support system. Write down your self-doubts and also what you're proud of doing every day. This will make it easier to love yourself. Learn to apologize to yourself when you treat yourself badly, and most importantly, don't hold back in doing what makes you happy.

Building Self-Compassion

Imagine your friend walks up to you and complains that she is making a lot of mistakes and doesn't think she's good enough. How would you respond? I'm sure you'd try to encourage and reassure her that it's okay to make mistakes. What if it were yourself in this scenario? Would you say the exact same thing to yourself?

Self-compassion is a positive attitude of treating yourself in a way that is forgiving, accepting, and loving. It's a way of embracing your ADHD and its challenges. Self-compassion can drive out your self-doubt. The good news is that you can learn and develop your own self-compassion.

A good place to start is by acknowledging your struggles and shortcomings without judgment; this will help you to find better strategies for resolving these struggles. Think of how you would treat your friends struggling with the same struggles and then extend the same empathy to yourself.

Accept that you are human, and being human comes with flaws—so instead of beating yourself up, eat something healthy, get up and take a walk, or even get yourself a massage. You deserve it.

Focus on the present and reduce your worries about the past and the future. Accept yourself for who you are. When you find yourself thinking a negative thought, turn it around and speak it out. You can try writing a letter to yourself about the situation without blaming anyone, including yourself.

Incorporating self-compassion takes time and patience to develop, so be gentle with yourself and don't give up. You are not alone in being imperfect.

Celebrating Small Wins

Small wins are so subtle that we may not even acknowledge them as accomplishments. They're easy to miss, especially if you are focusing on bigger wins. Waiting for a bigger accomplishment, however, might sometimes seem overwhelming or make us feel we are behind. Every small win adds up to a bigger achievement.

When we celebrate the small wins, the brain secretes dopamine, a "feel good" hormone that drives us to keep going. So the trick is to look out for what you achieve each day, no matter how little, and celebrate it. When you regularly acknowledge your wins, you are fighting self-doubt and imposter syndrome—and not only that, it will work to reinforce the idea that progress is possible Here are some strategies you can adopt to celebrate your small wins.

Write down the tasks you complete. This will help you get a clearer picture of what you've achieved each day and remind you that you are getting closer to your goal. Take time to reflect on your achievement and reward yourself. It might be as simple as taking a walk, buying yourself a flower, or treating yourself to your favorite TV show.

Share your accomplishments with supportive friends or family to keep you motivated. If it's too overwhelming, you can take a short break in between tasks. Be kind to yourself and remember that small wins are stepping stones to greater achievements, a confident future, and personal growth. Embrace them.

Enhancing Assertiveness and Self-Expression

Assertiveness is a way of expressing our feelings honestly and standing up for ourselves. It stems from the confidence of speaking your mind in a clear way while still respecting the rights of others.

Women are often faced with difficulty in being assertive and expressing themselves. Some find themselves being told what to do, having decisions made on their behalf, feeling pressured to say yes to inappropriate demands, and taking on everyone else's problems over their own, leading to others ignoring their wants or needs.

Being assertive is different from aggressiveness. An aggressive person ignores other people's feelings to get what they want and tries to win by bullying others. The goal of building assertiveness is to be self-confident, earn respect, manage stress, and make decisions on your own.

How can you enhance your assertiveness and self-expression?

Understand that you have the right to express your feelings and say 'no' without an apology or explanation. Learn to decline overwhelming tasks that go against your beliefs. Be firm, clear, and respectful and act confident when communicating.

Face the person directly, keep an upright posture, and don't cross your arms or legs. If it's difficult to say something, rehearse it beforehand in front of a mirror. You may also want to consider role-playing with your friends or colleagues. This will help you to feel more confident during the actual conversation.

Express your feelings by using 'I' statements to promote honest communication and to help you take ownership of your emotions. Be specific about what you want, but listen attentively without interruption before sharing your perspective.

Keep your tone in check to avoid conflict. You can practice deep breathing to help you remain calm and keep your voice firm. Ask for feedback from friends; this will help you to improve your assertiveness skills. Don't stop practicing—the payoff is worth the investment.

Body Positivity and ADHD

With ADHD, it is possible to fall into a trap of low self-esteem and self-criticism. This can lead some people to seek validation from others about things they can control—such as their body image. Studies have shown that many people with ADHD also suffer from body dysmorphic disorder (BDD).

BDD is a psychological condition characterized by a preoccupation with minor flaws in one's appearance. There may be compulsive behavior like unhealthy eating, comparing appearance to others, overexercising, cosmetic surgery, picking at skin, seeking validation about appearance, and many others.

The good news is that it is possible to embrace body positivity with ADHD.

How?

Be mindful of how you are thinking and talking about your body. Think of something good about your body and say it. If you can't find one, shift your focus to your body's strengths and capabilities. Don't assume that others are seeing you negatively. If you feel unsafe in your social circles or online, ditch the negative people and surround yourself with positive people.

Don't try to escape your ADHD traits by overfocusing on your body, and don't neglect your body either. When you catch yourself criticizing your body, challenge those thoughts. Are they based on facts or societal pressure? Replace negative self-talk with positive affirmations. Rather than focusing on appearance, appreciate what your body allows you to do. Can you dance, run, or simply breathe? Celebrate these abilities.

Media, and social media, often promote unrealistic body standards. Seek out body-positive role models and communities. Wear clothes that make you feel good about yourself, regardless of current trends. Recognize that beauty comes in all shapes, sizes, and colors. Appreciate the diversity of bodies around you. If social media is making you feel bad about your body, take a break or unfollow accounts that promote unhealthy body image.

Transforming Negative Self-Talk

Nurturing positive self-talk is important in building confidence. Previously, I highlighted self-talk as one major way of fighting self-doubt and imposter syndrome. Your self-talk indicates the way you perceive yourself and the world around you and even influences your decisions, so if you want to change things around you, it should start with your self-talk. Luckily, it is easy to implement.

How do you know that you're battling with negative self-talk? It's simple.

When you think of only the worst-case scenario, or when bad things happen outside your control and you believe they're your fault, that's an indicator of negative self-talk (for instance, blaming yourself for the failure of your group project or thinking it's your fault your friend is unhappy). Another is picking out only the negative things and filtering out the positive aspect of a situation.

Breaking free from negative self-talk requires commitment, hard work, and following the tips I'll be sharing here.

The first step in transforming your negative self-talk is to identify your negative patterns. This can be checked by reflecting on your thoughts and what you say. Keep a thought journal to get your thoughts on paper to help you identify recurring negative patterns and what triggers them.

Check through your negative self-talk and reframe it with new vocabulary—positive affirmations. Instead of saying, "I am always late," you can say, "I struggle with time management sometimes, but I can improve." The goal is not about putting a positive spin on every setback; it's to help you recognize that failure is a part of human nature and it's necessary for growth. Remind yourself of your achievements.

Practice self-compassion. Talk to yourself as you would talk to your friend. If things are too overwhelming, take a break; imagine yourself taking out your negative thought patterns and putting them in a box. You can revisit them with your support system or your therapist later.

Don't allow others to talk down to you. Protect yourself from their negative talk, whether by asking them to stop or separating yourself from them. This is where assertiveness comes in. Let go of those who don't treat you as you should be treated.

Here's a fun comparison of negative self-talk versus positive self-talk:

Scenario	Negative Self-Talk	Result of Negative Self-Talk	Positive Self-Talk	Result of Positive Self-Talk
Making a mistake at work	"I always mess up. I'm so useless."	Decreased confidence and increased anxiety	"Everyone makes mistakes. I can learn from this."	Improved confidence and resilience

Trying something new	"I'll never get this right. Why even try?"	Fear of failure and avoidance of new experiences	"It's okay to be a beginner. I'll get better with practice."	Increased willingness to try new things and learn
Receiving constructive feedback	"They think I'm terrible at my job."	Feeling demotivated and undervalued	"This feedback will help me improve. I can do better."	Feeling valued and motivated to improve
Facing a challenging task	"I'm not smart enough to handle this."	Reduced effort and giving up easily	"I can tackle this step by step. I've got this."	Increased effort and persistence
Looking in the mirror	"I look awful. I hate my body."	Low self-esteem and poor body image	"I am unique and beautiful just the way I am."	Improved self-esteem and body positivity
Social situations	"No one wants to talk to me. I'm so awkward."	Social anxiety and isolation	"I have interesting things to say and people like me."	Increased social confidence and engagement

Handling criticism	"I can't do anything right. I'm such a failure."	Decreased motivation and self-worth	"Criticism is a chance to grow. I'm capable of improvement."	Increased motivation and self-worth
Feeling overwhelmed	"I can't handle all this. I'm going to fail."	Increased stress and feelings of helplessness	"I can manage this one step at a time."	Reduced stress and a sense of control
Comparing to others	"I'll never be as good as them. I'm worthless."	Jealousy and decreased self-worth	"I have my own strengths and successes."	Appreciation of self and reduced jealousy
Trying to reach a goal	"I'm never going to make it. It's too hard."	Giving up on goals and feeling defeated	"I can achieve this if I keep working at it."	Persistence and a sense of accomplishment

Identifying and Using Your Unique Strengths

Women with ADHD are often misunderstood as weak, lazy, careless, less intelligent, or an embarrassment, and that's not true. Most people tend to obsess over their weaknesses, but like I mentioned earlier, it's not your fault you have ADHD; it's a result of your unique brain wiring—and because of this, you have many innate strengths which, if effectively channeled, can create a profound result.

What would happen if you were forced to do something that doesn't interest you? Would it be productive or produce the desired outcome? Certainly not!

Individuals with ADHD rely on their interests and strengths to drive productivity, but their strengths are often unrecognized due to the constant corrections and criticism they receive. However, you can maximize your energy and use your unique strengths effectively if you can identify them.

Recognizing these strengths will help you take ownership of your abilities and leverage them to develop your skills and build confidence. To identify your strengths, the first step is to identify activities or tasks that you enjoy doing. You can reflect on times you felt proud of yourself or received praise. Check for recurring patterns during these events and write down the skills you exhibited. You can ask friends, family, or colleagues to help you describe your strengths, or take a strengths assessment test to discover other strengths you may have overlooked.

Now that you have identified your strengths, the next step is to leverage them to develop your skills.

Remind yourself of your strengths and align them to your tasks and goals. Incorporate your strengths into your daily activities and give yourself the opportunity to use them regularly. You can also volunteer in roles that require you to use these strengths. You can work with people who complement your strengths to fill in the gaps where you may have weaknesses and help you develop complementary skills.

Worksheet: Daily Confidence Boost & Self-Compassion Tracker

Write down your top three personal strengths:

1. _____

2. _____

3. _____

Share three things you achieved today that made you proud, no matter how small:

_____

_____

_____

_____

Write a kind message to yourself.

I am _____

List three things you like about yourself and your appearance:

1. _____

2. _____

3. _____

List three things you are grateful for today:

1. _____

2. _____

3. _____

List three things you did to be kind to yourself:

1. _____

2. _____

3. _____

Write down one self-care activity you did today:

_____

_____

Takeaways

- For those with ADHD, the constant criticism and corrections they receive can lead to low self-esteem, low self-worth, imposter syndrome, and self-doubt. Building confidence around these areas can help with managing ADHD symptoms.

- Self-compassion means having a positive attitude and treating yourself in a way that is forgiving, accepting, and loving. It is a unique way of embracing your ADHD symptoms.

- Assertiveness is different from aggressiveness. It's a way of expressing your feelings honestly and clearly, with confidence, while respecting the rights of others.

We'd Love to Hear from You!

Dear Reader,

I hope you're enjoying this book as much as I enjoyed writing it. If the ideas and stories within these pages have resonated with you, inspired you, or simply provided a few moments of escape, I'd be honored if you'd share your thoughts with others.

Leaving a review on Amazon takes just a few seconds, but it can make a world of difference. Your feedback not only helps me grow as an author but also guides other readers in discovering books they'll truly connect with.

Option 1: Your review can help other readers discover their next favorite book. Click here to share your thoughts.

>> <u>Leave a review on Amazon US</u> <<

>> <u>Leave a review on Amazon UK</u> <<

Option 2: Scan the QR code below with your phone's camera to go directly to the review page.

>> Leave a review on Amazon US <<

>> Leave a review on Amazon UK <<

Thank you for taking the time to read this book, and thank you in advance for sharing your experience with the world.

Happy reading!

CHAPTER SIX

Cultivating Focus

"The ability to focus is a defining characteristic of successful individuals."

—Brian Tracy

"Let your eyes look straight ahead, And your eyelids look right before you. Ponder the path of your feet, And let all your ways be established. Do not turn to the right or the left; Remove your foot from evil."

—Proverbs 4:25-27 (NKJV)

Case Study

The clock was ticking really loud. It made me want to jump up and do something else. I was trying to read, but my eyes kept moving around. I couldn't stay focused on the page. My head was full of other stuff. I wanted to check my phone or do the dishes. It was hard to just sit still and read.

I shifted in my seat, trying to get comfortable, but it didn't help. The ticking seemed to grow louder, drowning out the words on the page. My thoughts raced, jumping from one thing to another. What did I need to do later? Did I remember to send that email?

I looked at the clock again, annoyed that only a few minutes had passed. The frustration built up inside me. I picked up my phone, hoping a quick *scroll would help me relax, but it only made things worse. Notifications kept coming up and soon enough, I was going from one app to another.*

The book lay open in front of me, untouched. I felt defeated. Why was something so simple so hard?

The Science of Attention

In psychology, attention means our ability to focus on one thing to the exclusion of everything else. Your brain uses a special system to pay attention, consisting of three main parts: alerting, orienting, and executive attention.

Alerting deals with getting ready to pay attention. When something grabs your interest, your brain prepares to focus, like when you hear a loud noise and instantly become alert. Your brain shifts gears from a relaxed state to one that is ready to take in new information. This alertness is the first step in paying attention and prepares you for deeper focus.

Once you're alert, your brain shifts into orienting. That is, you choose what to focus on. This might be a person talking, a book you're reading, or something you're looking at. Your brain uses signals from your eyes, ears, and other senses to figure out where to direct your attention. This helps you zero in on the most important or interesting thing in your environment.

Executive attention is understanding and processing what you're focusing on. After you've decided what to focus on, your brain's executive attention system takes over. This part of your brain helps you understand and think about the information you're focused on. It also helps you ignore distractions and stay focused on the task at hand. This process involves higher-level thinking and problem-solving skills.

When you pay attention, your brain makes stronger connections between neurons. This helps you learn and remember things better. For example, if you focus on learning a new language, your brain builds stronger connections for vocabulary and grammar.

Focusing on something over and over can change your brain's structure. This is called neuroplasticity. For example, musicians have bigger brain areas for hearing and moving their fingers because they practice a lot. When you repeatedly focus on a task or skill, your brain physically changes to become better at it. This means that with practice, you can actually improve your ability to pay attention and learn.

Attention is a key mental skill. It affects how we learn, remember, and interact with the world. Phones, social media, and trying to do many things at once make it hard to concentrate. Constant notifications and the urge to multitask can pull your attention in many directions at once, making it difficult to focus on any one thing for very long. This constant distraction can lead to problems with memory, learning, and even mental health as your brain struggles to keep up with the demands placed on it. Not to worry—I'll be showing you how you can master the art of paying attention even with ADHD.

Present-Moment Awareness

Present-moment awareness is the practice of focusing your attention on the here and now. That means you are fully engaged in the current moment, and you notice your thoughts, feelings, and surroundings without drawing a conclusion. This will help you reduce stress and also improve your mental clarity.

"Present moment" implies that you pay attention to what you are doing, feeling, and thinking *right now*, rather than getting caught up in past regrets or future worries. Notice your thoughts and feelings without judging them as good or bad, right or wrong.

One of the most significant benefits of present-moment awareness is its ability to reduce stress. When you avoid getting caught up in worries about the future or regrets about the past, it can help to lower levels of cortisol (the hormone associated with stress), leading to a calmer and more relaxed state of mind.

Practicing present-moment awareness trains your brain to concentrate better. This improved focus helps you perform tasks more efficiently and effectively so you can be fully engaged in what you are doing, make better decisions, and solve problems. This enhanced mental clarity helps in both professional and personal settings.

Paying attention to your breathing is a simple yet powerful way to anchor yourself in the present moment. Techniques like deep breathing (taking slow, deep breaths) and breath counting can help calm your mind and bring your focus back to the present.

You can also do a body scan. Lie down or sit comfortably and fix your attention on different parts of your body. You can start from your toes and move upwards. This practice helps you become more aware of physical sensations, which can ground you in the present moment and promote relaxation.

Other grounding techniques include simple activities like pressing your feet firmly on the ground, walking barefoot, or paying attention to the feel of an object in your hand. These techniques can be especially useful in moments of anxiety or stress.

When conversing with others, practice mindful listening by giving your full attention to the speaker. This involves not only hearing their words but also understanding their intentions and emotions. When you focus entirely on the other person, you can stay present in the interaction and build a deeper connection.

Eliminating Distractions

Distractions seem to be lurking around every corner, ready to derail our productivity and steal our precious time. There are constant notifications from social media, there's noise at work. Fortunately, there are foolproof methods to help you eliminate distractions and regain control of your attention.

The first step is to identify whether your distractions are external, like loud noises or interruptions from colleagues, or internal, such as daydreaming or stress. Spend a day or two observing what typically distracts you. Keep a journal to note down every time you get sidetracked. This exercise will help you become more aware of your distraction triggers.

Having a dedicated workspace can also help you reduce distractions. Choose a quiet, comfortable spot where you can work without interruptions. Make sure your workspace is well-organized and free from clutter. I prefer a clean and tidy environment that helps me focus better and reduces the temptation to procrastinate.

Setting clear goals and prioritizing tasks can provide a roadmap for your day, helping you stay focused on what's important. Use tools like to-do lists, planners, or digital apps to keep track of and prioritize your tasks.

Let me give you a time management technique that works. It's called the Pomodoro technique, and it involves working for a set period, typically 25 minutes, followed by a short break. This method helps you to sustain concentration and have regular breaks, preventing burnout and keeping distractions at bay.

Now, let's talk about one of the major distractions we all face: our mobile phones. To combat this, set specific times to check your emails and social media. Turn off non-essential notifications, and use apps or features on your phone that block distracting websites during work hours.

Stress can be another major distraction. When you're stressed, it's difficult to concentrate on your tasks. Find ways to manage stress, as this will help you maintain your productivity. Exercise, proper nutrition, and adequate sleep will all help.

Setting boundaries with others can minimize interruptions. Let your colleagues, friends, and family know when you're working and shouldn't be disturbed. Use signals like closing your office door or wearing headphones to indicate that you're in a focused work mode. Establishing these boundaries can help create a more distraction-free environment.

Finally, multitasking might seem like a good way to get more done, but it often leads to decreased productivity and more distractions. Focus on one task at a time and give it your full attention. This approach, known as single-tasking, can improve the quality of your work and help you complete tasks more efficiently.

Eliminating distractions is a continuous process that requires self-awareness and discipline. Stay committed, and soon you'll find yourself working more efficiently and with greater ease.

Chunking and Sequencing

Whether you're trying to remember a grocery list, organize a project at work, or learn a new skill, you need to learn how to process and retain information. Chunking and sequencing aid in memory retention and also enhance our ability to stay organized and focused. Let's talk about how chunking and sequencing work and how you can use them to your advantage.

Chunking is a technique that involves breaking down large pieces of information into smaller, more manageable units, or "chunks." This method makes it easier for your brain to process and remember information. Think of chunking as a way to simplify complex data by grouping related items together.

There are various examples of chunking in our day to day living. For example, for phone numbers, instead of remembering a long string of numbers (e.g., 1234567890), you break it down into chunks (e.g., 123-456-7890). With grocery lists, instead of recalling a long list of items individually, you group them into categories (e.g., fruits, vegetables, dairy).

When you break information into chunks, you reduce cognitive overload, making it easier to store and recall data. Chunking helps you concentrate on one group of information at a time, reducing distractions and enhancing focus. This technique streamlines the learning process, allowing you to process information more quickly and effectively.

How about sequencing? Sequencing is the process of arranging information or tasks in a logical order. This method helps you understand and remember the steps needed to complete a task or the order of events in a process. Sequencing is particularly useful in activities that require following a set of instructions or understanding the flow of a narrative.

For example, following the steps in a recipe in the correct order ensures the dish turns out as intended. Organizing tasks in a project according to priority makes it easier for you to complete them on time. Breaking down a new skill into sequential steps can make the learning process more manageable and less overwhelming. Sequencing helps organize information in a logical manner, making it easier to follow and understand.

Combining chunking and sequencing can significantly improve your ability to manage and remember information. So, how do you chunk and sequence? Start by identifying the information you need to remember or organize. This could be anything from a to-do list to something more complex.

Next, group related items together into chunks. For example, if you're working on a project, group tasks by their category or priority. If you're studying, group related concepts or topics together.

Once you have your chunks, arrange them in a logical sequence. You can choose the order in which tasks need to be completed. This sequencing will help you understand the flow of information and ensure nothing is overlooked.

Take time to periodically review and revise your chunks and sequences. As you go on, you may find that certain chunks need to be rearranged or additional steps need to be added to the sequence. Stay flexible to stay effective.

Turning High Energy into Productive Outcomes

A high-energy state can be a double-edged sword. On one hand, it can lead to incredible achievements; on the other, it can cause distraction and inefficiency. So, how do you harness this energy effectively? High energy can show up in different ways: enthusiasm, restlessness, or a constant need to be doing something. While it can be overwhelming, especially with ADHD, it can also be a big advantage when directed correctly. The key is to understand your energy patterns and learn how to manage them to your advantage.

First and foremost, accept that having high energy is a part of who you are. Instead of seeing it as a hindrance, consider it an advantage. One of the most effective ways to channel high energy is to set clear, achievable goals. Goals give your energy a direction and purpose. Start by identifying what you want to achieve, whether it's completing a project, learning a new skill, or improving your fitness. Break these goals down into smaller tasks to maintain focus and motivation. I talked about setting goals earlier; you can flip back for a little revision.

A structured routine will give you the framework needed to make use of that high-energy productively. Establish a daily schedule that includes time for work, exercise, relaxation, and hobbies. Consistency helps create a rhythm, making it easier to manage your energy levels. With high energy, it's easy to jump from one task to another, and that leads to unfinished projects and frustration. Prioritizing tasks ensures that your energy is spent on the most important activities first.

Identify your strengths and find ways to leverage them. With your high energy, you are likely to do well in dynamic, fast-paced environments. Rather than trying to fit into the mold, you can look for projects that align with your natural abilities and interests.

Managing Hyperfocus

When you are hyperfocused (paying intense attention to only one thing or activity), you might lose track of time, become completely absorbed, and excel at the task at hand. While this can lead to high productivity and creativity, it can also result in neglecting other obligations and becoming unbalanced.

On one side, hyperfocus allows you to fully concentrate on tasks, leading to high-quality work, breakthroughs, and innovation. Hyperfocus creates high motivation, which can drive you to achieve significant goals.

On the flip side, intense focus on one task can make you overlook other important duties and make it difficult to gauge how much time has passed, potentially leading to missed deadlines or appointments. Extended periods of hyperfocus can result in burnout and mental exhaustion.

To cope with hyperfocus, establish specific time limits for tasks. Use timers or alarms to remind you when it's time to switch tasks or take breaks. For example, you can set a timer for 60 minutes and then take a 5-10 minute break. This helps prevent you from getting lost in a task and ensures that other responsibilities are also addressed.

Develop a balanced schedule that includes time for various activities and responsibilities (work, exercise, social activities, etc.) to reduce the risk of becoming overly absorbed in one task.

Another key strategy is to identify and prioritize tasks and address the most important responsibilities first. Use to-do lists or task management apps to keep track of priorities.

Schedule regular check-ins with yourself or with a colleague to review your progress and ensure that you're staying on track. These check-ins can help you reassess your priorities and adjust your focus as needed.

Last tip before moving on: Create a strategy for transitioning between tasks. For example, use a short routine or ritual to signal the end of one task and the beginning of another. This helps you shift your focus more smoothly and maintain balance between different responsibilities.

Procrastination in ADHD

In women with ADHD, procrastination is not just about putting things off; it's often tied to deeper issues, such as difficulty with time management, motivation, and emotional regulation. Why does procrastination happen in ADHD? With ADHD, there is usually a struggle to manage time effectively. This stems from an impaired sense of time, which makes it hard to gauge how long tasks will take or how to prioritize them.

Furthermore, as we discussed in an earlier chapter, ADHD typically impairs executive functions like planning and organizing as well as emotional regulation. This can lead to difficulties in breaking tasks into manageable steps or create feelings of overwhelm, resulting in procrastination.

Let me go a step further—for women with ADHD, motivation is driven by immediate rewards rather than long-term goals. It's easier to cook something simple knowing you'll quickly have a delicious meal to eat than stick with a three-month healthy eating meal plan. Tasks that don't provide instant gratification can be harder to start and complete, leading to procrastination.

Breaking the Procrastination Cycle

I've also had my own share of being stuck in procrastination. For instance, I would often find myself putting off writing an important email until the last minute, only to end up rushing through it and making careless mistakes. Too many days, I convinced myself that cleaning my room could wait just one more hour. But the more I procrastinated, the more I felt as though I was living below my best. It felt as though I could be functioning at 100%, but I remained stuck at 20%.

Procrastination is a relentless cycle that's hard to break. The more you delay tasks, the more overwhelmed you become, which can make starting even more difficult. If you're stuck in this cycle, don't worry—there are practical strategies you can use to regain control and boost your productivity.

The procrastination cycle starts when you get overwhelmed by all the things you need to do. This feeling leads to avoidance, which gives you temporary relief but ultimately increases stress as deadlines approach.

This cycle of delay and stress can continue, making it difficult to break free and do what you need to do.

To break free, you need to identify the exact reason you keep procrastinating. Common causes include fear of failure, perfectionism, or lack of interest. Next thing is to break down what you need to do into smaller steps (remember chunking?). Instead of setting a goal of "complete project," try "draft outline," "write first section," and "edit draft." When you set specific and achievable goals, the tasks feel less overwhelming, helping you to make steady progress.

You can also use the two-minute rule: If a task takes less than two minutes, do it immediately. This rule helps you overcome inertia and reduces the number of small tasks that can pile up and contribute to procrastination.

Procrastination often involves harsh self-judgment and guilt. Be patient with yourself and give yourself some grace. I just shared my own struggle; there are a lot of other people out there who also struggle with procrastination. Instead of criticizing yourself, focus on what you can do to improve and take proactive steps to address the issue. You can set up a reward system for every time you do what you're supposed to do at the time you're supposed to do it. Rewards could be a short break, a treat, or even phone time. This positive reinforcement will encourage you to stay on track.

Time Management Techniques

You've got a million things going on. Work, family, maybe some hobbies, and let's not forget *you* time. It's like trying to juggle chainsaws while baking a cake. Women often end up doing the lion's share of housework and childcare as well, which is like having a second full-time job. Managing your time well helps you balance this invisible workload.

Time management will also help your career. It shows you can handle pressure, meet deadlines, and still have a life. When you're in control of your time, you're less stressed and more chill. Want to spend quality time with your loved ones? You need to make time for them. Time management helps you prioritize relationships without feeling guilty.

Everyone needs time to recharge. Whether it's reading or binge-watching your favorite show, managing your time ensures you get those precious moments. When you're not rushing around like a chicken with its head cut off, you're more productive and less stressed. Managing your time can help you manage your money as well since you'll have more time to budget, save, and avoid impulse buys. Feeling in control of your time is empowering.

The first step to getting a hold of your time is to understand your own unique patterns and preferences. Are you a morning person who prefers an early start, or do you find your focus peaks in the afternoon? By identifying your peak productivity times, you can schedule demanding tasks accordingly. Additionally, consider your energy levels throughout the day. Certain tasks might drain your energy while others rejuvenate you.

Plan and prioritize. Effective time management hinges on careful planning and prioritization. Start by setting clear goals, both short-term and long-term. Break down large goals into smaller, actionable steps to make them less overwhelming. Creating to-do lists can be helpful, but you need to choose what's most important. Differentiate between urgent tasks (those demanding immediate attention) and important tasks (those that contribute to your long-term goals). Focus on high-impact activities that align with your priorities.

You can also try batch processing, which involves grouping similar tasks together and completing them in one go. For example, dedicate a specific time each day to handling emails or completing routine administrative tasks. This reduces context-switching and increases efficiency.

A well-structured schedule is a cornerstone of effective time management. Consider implementing time blocking, where you dedicate specific time blocks for different activities or tasks. This can help you maintain focus and avoid distractions. It's also essential to build flexibility into your schedule. Unforeseen events happen, so having some buffer time can prevent stress. Short breaks can actually boost productivity by helping you recharge and refocus.

Be Patient

I know patience is not exactly the most exciting topic, but hear me out. If you're a woman with ADHD, you probably know that patience isn't exactly your middle name. Between the racing thoughts, the impulsive nature, and that general feeling of being five steps ahead of everyone else, waiting can feel like torture.

So, why is patience even important? Well, for starters, it can save you from accidentally saying something you'll regret. It can help you build stronger relationships by giving you time to really listen to others, which people truly appreciate—it shows that you value their opinions. And let's be real, it can make your life a whole lot less stressful.

When you're patient, you're more likely to think things through before acting. This can lead to better decisions and fewer regrets. Patience gives your brain time to come up with creative solutions. You're less likely to get stuck in one way of thinking.

Mastering patience helps you build self-control in other areas of your life. When you slow down and savor the moment, you're more likely to appreciate the little things. Patience is a muscle you can build. The more you practice it, the stronger it gets.

So, while patience might not always be easy, it's definitely worth the effort. But how do you actually be patient? I know you're likely used to being in the fast lane. But sometimes, it's okay to slow down and enjoy the ride.

Let's talk about your brain (again!). Your brain is like a super-fast computer, but sometimes it goes into overdrive. When you're feeling impatient, it's like your brain is hitting the fast-forward button. So, how do you slow it down? Well, one way is to focus on the here and now, instead of worrying about what's next. Try taking a few deep breaths or counting to ten. It might sound simple, but it really works.

Another thing you can do is to change your habits. If you're always rushing around, try to slow down a bit. Give yourself extra time to get places, or take a break when you're feeling overwhelmed. And remember, it's okay to say no. Overcommitting yourself is a surefire way to feel stressed and impatient.

Worksheet: Focused Work Session Log

Here is a focused work session log to help you stay calm and focused on whatever activity you're doing. You can use it again and again. I'll give you a scenario on how to use the log, then leave blank spaces for you to fill out.

Lynn is a freelance writer who wants to stay focused. She has a big article deadline coming up. To stay on track, she uses this focused work session log.

Date: July 30, 2024

Time Started: 2:00 PM

Time Ended: 4:00 PM

Total Time: 2 hours

Task/Goal:

Write the first draft of an article on "The Benefits of Remote Work"

Environment:

Quiet home office, slight noise from the street outside

Steps taken: Closed the window, used noise-canceling headphones, activated a website blocker for social media

Focus Level:

Rating: 4

Productivity:

Goal Achieved: Yes!

Progress: Wrote 1,200 words, outlined the remaining sections

Challenges:

Obstacle: Distraction due to a delivery

Solution: Took a quick break to receive the package and then refocused by re-reading the last paragraph written

Lessons Learned:

Worked Well: Headphones and website blocker were very effective

Improvement: Need a better plan for potential interruptions—maybe a "Do Not Disturb" sign on the door next time

By using the worksheet, Lynn stayed organized, minimized distractions, and completed a significant portion of her article. Plus, she now has a better plan for managing future interruptions.

Why not try it out for yourself?

Date: _____

Time Started: _____

Time Ended: _____

Total Time: _____

Task/Goal:

Clearly define the specific task or goal for this session.

_____

_____

_____

_____

_____

_____

Environment:

Describe your work environment (quiet, noisy, distractions present).

_____

_____

_____

_____

_____

_____

Note any steps taken to minimize distractions (e.g., noise-canceling headphones, website blockers).

_____

_____

_____

_____

_____

Focus Level:

Rate your focus level on a scale of 1-5 (1 = very low, 5= very high).

_____ 1

_____ 2

_____ 3

_____ 4

_____ 5

Productivity:

Assess task completion: Did you achieve your goal?

Yes/No

Challenges:

Identify obstacles encountered during the session.

_____

_____

_____

_____

_____

Describe how you handled these challenges or plan to address them in future.

_____

_____

_____

_____

_____

Lessons Learned:

Reflect on what worked well and what could be improved for future sessions.

_____

_____

_____

_____

_____

Additional Notes:

Any other thoughts or observations from the session?

_____

_____

_____

_____

_____

Takeaways

- When you pay attention, your brain makes stronger connections between neurons. This helps you learn and remember things better. For example, if you focus on learning a new language, your brain builds stronger connections for vocabulary and grammar.

- The first step in eliminating distractions is to identify what they are. Distractions can be external, like loud noises or interruptions from colleagues, or internal, such as daydreaming or stress.

- Combining chunking and sequencing can significantly improve your ability to manage and remember information.

- Mastering patience helps you build self-control in other areas of your life. When you slow down and savor the moment, you're more likely to appreciate the little things. Patience can reduce stress, which is great for your overall health. The more you practice patience, the easier it gets.

CHAPTER SEVEN

Coping with Common Challenges

"Strength doesn't come from what you can do. It comes from overcoming the things you once thought you couldn't."

—Rikki Rogers

"Fear not, for I am with you; Be not dismayed, for I am your God. I will strengthen you, Yes, I will help you, I will uphold you with My righteous right hand."

—Isaiah 41:10 (NKJV)

Case Study

I feel like I'm drowning. Not in water, but in expectations. The world sees a mom—someone in control, calm, and collected. But that's not me. My mind races like a squirrel on a treadmill, jumping from one thought to another. And my kids? They're always active and jumpy.

People look at me like I'm failing. Like my kids' wildness is my fault. It's not. We're just different. It's like trying to fit a square peg in a round hole.

I try so hard. I make rules, stick to schedules, and ask for help. But it's like chasing a rainbow. It's always just out of reach. The house is a mess, the kids are climbing the walls, and I'm exhausted.

Sometimes I just want to disappear. To run away and hide. But I can't. I love my kids too much. So I keep going, one day at a time, hoping that one day people will understand. That they'll see the real me, not the perfect mom they expect.

Managing Time Blindness in Personal and Professional Life

Ever feel like time is playing tricks on you? You sit down to write a quick email and suddenly it's dusk, and you haven't showered (oops!). This, my friend, is time blindness. Time blindness describes the inability to accurately judge how much time has passed or how long tasks will take. It's like your internal clock runs on a different time zone than the rest of the world. While anyone can experience it, some studies suggest it might be more common in women. Maybe it's the mental juggling act of work, family, and that never-ending to-do list?

Some theories suggest a disconnect in the brain that makes it difficult to interpret cues like light changes or hunger pangs, which usually signal time passing. Others point to conditions like ADHD, which can impact focus and time management.

Being chronically late, missing deadlines, and feeling constantly rushed are common side effects of being time blind. This time trouble can seep into every area of your life, from work to relationships. It can lead to stress, guilt, and even missed opportunities. So, how do you conquer time blindness and reclaim control of your schedule?

Let's start off with time tracking. Time tracking is like a financial audit for your day. Take time to go through how you spent your day. Jot whatever details you have down. By writing down how you spend your hours, you can see where your time really goes. It's like finding those mysterious charges on your credit card—except instead of dollars, you're tracking minutes.

Why bother? Knowing where your time vanishes can make a world of difference. Maybe you discover you spend hours scrolling through social media or get sucked into endless email vortexes. With this information, you can reallocate time to more productive or enjoyable activities.

To track, you can use apps as well as journals. Choose what suits you. For a week, note down every 30 minutes or every hour what you're doing. Be honest—even watching cat videos counts.

One other way to deal with time blindness is to learn to say no. Overcommitting is stressful, and it's not doing you any favors. Your time is valuable. Saying yes to everything leaves you stretched thin and unable to give your best to anything. It's like trying to juggle ten balls—something's bound to drop.

Be direct and polite. A simple, "I appreciate the offer, but I'm unable to commit at this time" is effective. You can also set boundaries. Clearly communicate your limits. "I'm too busy right now" is better than feeling overwhelmed. Or you can offer alternatives. Suggest another person or time if appropriate. It shows you're considering their request. Saying no gets easier with practice. Start now and build confidence with time. For example, if a friend asks you to hang out every weekend, instead of saying yes out of obligation, try, "I'd love to spend more time with you, but weekends are family time. How about we meet for coffee next week?"

Strategies for Dealing with Overwhelm and Burnout

Overwhelm is the feeling of being overstimulated and overloaded. It's like trying to juggle lit candlesticks while blindfolded. Burnout, on the other hand, is the emotional and physical exhaustion that comes from prolonged stress and overwhelm. It's like the candlesticks have fallen, and you're too tired to pick them up.

Overwhelm and burnout often stem from a combination of factors. Let's break down some common culprits. The first is having too much on your plate. Constant deadlines and a seemingly endless to-do list create a sense of urgency that's hard to escape.

Our hyper-connected world blurs the lines between work and personal life. Constant notifications and the pressure to be available 24/7 leave little time to recharge. When life feels chaotic and unpredictable, it's easy to feel overwhelmed. Lack of control over circumstances can lead to a sense of helplessness. Striving for flawless results is exhausting. The fear of making mistakes hinders progress and creates unnecessary stress.

Lack of support can make challenges feel insurmountable. Prioritizing work or others over your own needs leads to burnout. When your basic needs aren't met, your ability to cope with stress diminishes.

To overcome overwhelm and burnout, you can try out physical activity. Whether it's hitting the gym, going for a run, or even dancing, physical activity releases endorphins and boosts your mood. Also, what you eat and how much sleep you get directly impact your energy levels and ability to cope with stress. Go for nutrient-rich foods and aim for 7-9 hours of quality sleep each night.

What do you enjoy doing? Engaging in hobbies will give you a much-needed escape from daily stressors. So, if you enjoy painting, paint. If you prefer to watch movies, why not? Just ensure you allocate time for it. I'd like to add that spending time outdoors has been shown to reduce stress and improve mood. Even a short walk around your neighborhood can help you relieve stress.

In addition to these, you can do a digital detox. Take regular breaks from screens. This can help reduce information overload and give your mind a rest. Laugh. Laughter is truly the best medicine. Watch funny movies, spend time with your friends, or listen to comedy podcasts.

The Impulsivity Spectrum

Impulsivity isn't a black and white thing. It's more like a rainbow, with everyone experiencing it in different shades. On one end, you have occasional impulsive urges that you can usually manage. On the other end, impulsivity can be more severe and disruptive to daily life.

Impulsivity has some common signs: you act first, think later; decisions are made at lightning speed, sometimes leading to regretted choices; and there is also impulse-buying. Shiny new thing? Must. Have. It! You almost can't deny the thrill of instant gratification.

Another telltale sign is talking too much. Yes, that's right—you blurt out thoughts before filtering them, sometimes leading to awkward silences or hurt feelings. You struggle to sit still or focus for extended periods, always needing a change of pace.

And there's more. The impulsivity spectrum isn't just about outward behaviors; it can also affect how you manage emotions and handle relationships. For example, someone on the impulsive side is likely to have trouble regulating anger. A short fuse will make you easily frustrated, leading to frequent outbursts. You may also make impulsive relationship decisions, falling head over heels in love (or out of it) at breakneck speed.

It isn't all bad. Impulsivity can be a double-edged sword. While it can lead to some not-so-good scenarios, it also comes with some perks. For one, you easily accept life's unexpected turns. Your impulsive nature can also help with creativity. You don't get stuck in analysis paralysis—you just go for it!

To ensure things stay in check, you can take a beat before responding. Even a few seconds can make a difference in making a wise choice. Also, think about what triggers the impulsivity. What situations or emotions make you more impulsive? Figure it out and monitor them, then plan ahead on how to deal with these impulses before they show up.

Impulse Control Techniques

As I mentioned earlier, there are two sides to impulsivity. While it fuels spontaneity and quick action, it can also lead to rash decisions and regretted actions. So, how do you ensure that impulsivity remains an advantage for you?

I mentioned triggers earlier. What situations or emotions make you more susceptible to acting impulsively? For example, when you're stressed and frustrated, the urge to react impulsively can be stronger than usual. The same applies when you are bored. You can impulsively look for a quick fix, leading to you acting impulsively to fill the void.

Also, when you're mentally or physically drained, your self-control weakens. Consider shopping malls, casinos, and other environments loaded with temptation as high risk.

What do you do once you've been able to isolate the triggers? Take a step back. Before reacting, take a few seconds (or even minutes) to calm down and assess the situation. Consider the potential consequences of your actions.

One more thing: don't wait for the heat of the moment to develop strategies. When you feel an impulse brewing, have a list of healthy alternatives at hand. This could be going for a walk, listening to some good music (I absolutely love country—try it out!), or calling a friend.

Create "if-then" statements. Develop mental roadmaps for common situations. For example, "If I feel stressed at work, then I will take a five-minute walk and do some deep breathing exercises." That helps you plan ahead and stay on top of impulsivity. If impulsive online shopping is a problem, consider browser extensions that block shopping websites during certain times.

Impulse control is a skill that can be strengthened with practice. When you resist an impulsive urge and make a conscious choice, praise yourself. Reflect on your impulsive behaviors. What were the triggers? How did you feel afterward? Tracking these patterns can help you identify areas for improvement.

Simplifying Household Management for ADHD Minds

ADHD makes it hard to stay focused on one task. Your mind wanders; you start one thing but end up doing something else. This makes it hard to finish chores. Not to mention how easy it is to get overwhelmed by the clutter and mess.

Another problem is remembering things. You might forget to buy milk or pay a bill. This can cause extra stress and make it harder to keep the house running smoothly.

But don't worry, there are ways to make things easier. The most important thing is to be kind to yourself. It's okay if your house isn't perfect all the time. Start small. Don't try to clean the whole house at once. Pick one small area, like a drawer or a shelf, and focus on that. Once you finish, give yourself a short break.

Find a home for everything. This might sound simple, but it really helps. When you know where things belong, it's easier to put them away. Use boxes, baskets, or shelves to keep things organized.

Use labels. Labeling things can help you remember where everything goes. This is especially helpful when you have ADHD. Ask for help. Don't be afraid to ask family or friends for help. Even a little bit of help can make a big difference. Establish consistent daily routines for tasks like making the bed, doing dishes, and tidying up. This can help create a sense of structure.

Create a schedule for more intensive cleaning tasks like vacuuming, dusting, and bathroom cleaning. Breaking things down can make them less overwhelming. Use containers of different sizes to organize everything from pantry items to toys. Labeling containers and shelves can help you quickly find what you need and put things away efficiently.

Regularly go through your belongings and get rid of anything you don't need or use. A clutter-free space is easier to maintain. Involve your family. Let them handle specific household chores. You can even create a chore chart to help everyone know their specific responsibilities. Make it fun. Turn cleaning into a game or challenge to make it more enjoyable.

Developing Financial Management Skills

Financial management might sound serious, but it's inevitable. With good financial skills, you can make informed decisions, support yourself, and feel independent. Knowing your finances helps you make better career choices. Whether you're negotiating a raise or starting your own business, having a grip on your money means you're always a step ahead. Life throws us unexpected surprises, and having a financial cushion can make these moments easier to work through.

Want to travel the world, buy a home, or go back to school? Managing your finances well can help turn these dreams into reality. Your goals are within reach with a solid financial plan. Remember, you're a role model to those around you, especially your kids. When you manage your money wisely, you're setting a great example and teaching lessons about financial responsibility.

Money worries are a major stressor. By keeping your finances in check, you can reduce anxiety and enjoy a more peaceful, worry-free life. Understanding finances means you can advocate for fair wages and benefits. You'll feel more confident negotiating and standing up for what you deserve.

Start by tracking your income and expenses. Understanding where your money goes each month is the first step in taking control of your finances. Use budgeting apps or simple spreadsheets to keep things organized. A budget doesn't restrict your spending; rather, it helps you make sure your money is working for you.

Your credit score can affect everything from loan approvals to interest rates. Regularly check your credit report and address any discrepancies. Good credit management includes paying bills on time, keeping credit card balances low, and avoiding unnecessary debt.

Investing can seem like a big deal, but it's an effective way to grow your wealth. Start with understanding basic investment options like stocks, bonds, and mutual funds. You can consult a financial advisor to create an investment strategy that aligns with your goals and risk tolerance. Financial literacy is key to effective financial management. Take advantage of online courses, workshops, and books to deepen your understanding of personal finance. The more you know, the better decisions you'll make.

Not all debt is bad, but you need to know how to manage your debts wisely. Prioritize paying off high-interest debts first and consider consolidating your debts to lower your interest rates. Avoid accumulating new debt unless it's for an investment that will pay off in the long run.

It's never too early to start planning for retirement. Take advantage of retirement accounts like 401(k)s or IRAs and contribute regularly. Employer matching programs can also boost your savings, so don't leave that money on the table. Ensure you have adequate health, life, and property insurance to protect yourself and your family from unforeseen events.

Mindful Decision-Making

Making decisions can sometimes feel overwhelming, especially when there are many options or significant consequences. Before making any decision, take a moment to pause and breathe deeply. This simple act helps to clear your mind and bring your focus to the present moment. When you're stressed or hurried, your decisions can be reactive rather than thoughtful. Take a few deep breaths to calm your nervous system and create space for more deliberate thinking. This brief pause can make a significant difference in how you approach the decision.

Knowing what truly matters will help you make mindful decisions. Reflect on your core values and let them guide your choices. When your decisions align with your values, you're more likely to feel content and at peace with the outcomes. For instance, if one of your core values is family, consider how each option will affect your loved ones. This reflection helps to ensure that your decisions are beneficial not only in the short term but also in the long run.

Instead of rushing to a conclusion, take the time to consider all your options. Write them down if that helps you visualize them better. Look at the potential outcomes of each option and how they align with your goals and values. This thorough examination allows you to see the bigger picture and avoid impulsive decisions.

Listen to your gut. Your intuition is powerful and it helps you know what's best for you before your rational mind does. Pay attention to how you feel about each option. Sometimes, your gut feeling can even give you an idea of what logical analysis might miss. Trusting your intuition doesn't mean ignoring facts or data; it means considering your inner feelings as part of the decision-making process. This balance between intuition and logic can lead you to more satisfying and holistic decisions.

While your decision is ultimately yours to make, ask for input from those around you. Talk to friends, family members, or colleagues who might have experience or insights related to your decision. However, you still have to balance their advice with your own judgment and values. Sometimes, a fresh perspective can show you something you hadn't considered, but it's essential to filter this input through the lens of your own priorities and circumstances.

Creating a simple pros and cons list for each option can be incredibly helpful. This method allows you to see the benefits and drawbacks of each choice clearly. You can weigh the pros and cons against each other and make a more informed decision. This analytical approach complements the more intuitive aspects of mindful decision-making, providing a well-rounded perspective on your options.

Finally, let go of perfection. Perfectionism can be paralyzing and counterproductive in decision-making. Understand that no decision is without risk or uncertainty. Focus on making the best choice with the information you have rather than seeking a flawless outcome. This mindset shift can reduce anxiety and help you move forward more decisively.

Long-Term Planning

The first step in long-term planning is to define your vision. What do you want your life to look like in 5, 10, or even 20 years? Take some time to dream big and think about your ideal future. This could include career aspirations, personal milestones, financial goals, or even lifestyle choices. Having a clear vision gives you a target to aim for and makes the planning process more focused and meaningful.

Think of your goals as destinations on a map. Now, you need to create a roadmap to reach them. This involves breaking down your long-term goals into steps. For instance, if your goal is to save for a house, your roadmap might include creating a budget, cutting unnecessary expenses, setting up a savings account, and researching mortgage options. Each step brings you closer to your ultimate goal.

I can't emphasize enough how important it is to prioritize what matters most. Recognize that you might need to adjust your priorities along the way. Make a list of your goals and rank them by importance. Focus on one or two major goals at a time to avoid feeling overwhelmed. It's okay to revisit and revise your plans as circumstances change. Good planning requires consistent effort and time management. Set aside regular time—weekly or monthly—to review your goals and assess your progress. This helps you stay accountable and make necessary adjustments to your plan.

No plan is without hitches. Anticipating potential obstacles can help you stay prepared and resilient. Think about what could go wrong and how you can mitigate these risks. For example, if you're planning a career change, consider the skills you need to acquire and the financial cushion you might need during the transition. Have contingency plans in place to ensure you're not caught off guard.

Your long-term plan should be firm but not entirely rigid. Regularly review and adjust your plan to ensure it remains relevant and aligned with your goals. Life changes, and so should your plans. By staying flexible and responsive to new information and circumstances, you can keep your long-term vision on track.

Worksheet: Impulse Control Log

This impulse control log will help you track your impulses and develop better self-control. Let's get started.

1. Date: _____

2. Time: _____

3. Describe the impulse:

(What was the impulse? For example, "I wanted to eat a chocolate bar even though I'm on a diet.")

_____

_____

_____

_____

_____

4. Situation:

(Where were you and what were you doing when you had the impulse? For example, "I was at the office, feeling stressed.")

_____

_____

_____

_____

_____

5. Trigger:

(What might have triggered this impulse? For example, "I was feeling overwhelmed with work deadlines.")

_____

_____

_____

_____

6. Emotional state:

(How did you feel when you experienced the impulse? For example, "I felt anxious and tired.")

- Calm
- Anxious
- Frustrated
- Bored
- Sad
- Other: _____

7. Response:

(How did you react to the impulse? For example, "I resisted the urge and went for a walk instead.")

_____

_____

_____

_____

8. Outcome:

(What was the result of your response? For example, "I felt better after the walk and was able to refocus on my work.")

_____

_____

_____

_____

_____

9. Reflection:

(What did you learn from this experience? For example, "I realized that taking a break helps me manage my stress better.")

_____

_____

_____

_____

10. Action plan:

(What strategies can you use in the future to handle similar impulses? For example, "Next time I feel overwhelmed, I'll take a short break or do a quick breathing exercise.")

_____

_____

_____

_____

Here is a table to help you quickly fill out your impulses and situations surrounding them. You can save it on our phone and keep a record on the go:

Date	Situation	Impulse Triggered	Reaction	Afterthoughts	What Could I Do Differently?

Takeaways

- Being chronically late, missing deadlines, and feeling constantly rushed are common side effects of being time blind. This time trouble can seep into every area of your life, from work to relationships. It can lead to stress, guilt, and even missed opportunities.

- Impulse control is a skill that can be strengthened with practice. When you resist an impulsive urge and make a conscious choice, praise yourself.

- When it comes to organizing your living space, find a home for everything. This might sound simple, but it really helps. When you know where things belong, it's easier to put them away. Use boxes, baskets, or shelves to keep things organized.

- Let go of perfection. Perfectionism can be paralyzing and counterproductive in decision-making. Understand that no decision is without risk or uncertainty.

PART THREE

Unleashing Your ADHD Superpowers

W hat if you could be Superwoman? Large muscles, shooting fire from your eyes, and the ability to fly. That'd be pretty awesome, right? While you might not be able to grow wings or bench-press a car, you can be just as extraordinary.

A brain that's always on, buzzing with ideas and connections; the ability to hyperfocus on a task until it's complete. These aren't weaknesses, they're superpowers in disguise. They're like a built-in turbocharger for your creativity and problem-solving skills.

So, instead of seeing ADHD as a limitation, let's reframe it as a superpower waiting to be unleashed. It's time to stop apologizing for your brain and start celebrating its extraordinary capabilities.

CHAPTER EIGHT

Improving Interpersonal Relationships

❧

"Love recognizes no barriers. It jumps hurdles, leaps fences, penetrates walls to arrive at its destination full of hope."

—Maya Angelou

"And be kind to one another, tenderhearted, forgiving one another, even as God in Christ forgave you."

—Ephesians 4:32 (NKJV)

Case Study

I was blindsided. A text? Really? Ben and I had shared laughter, tears, and countless inside jokes. Now it was over, condensed into a few cold lines on a screen. The realization hit me like a ton of bricks. Was it my fault? My mind replayed countless moments, searching for clues. I'd always thought I was just a little clumsy, a bit forgetful. But now, with this gaping hole in my life, I wondered if there was something more to it.

Work was a different kind of hell. Meetings were a blur of faces and voices. My mind would wander, chasing squirrels of random thoughts. People would look at me like I was from another planet when I'd blurt out something completely off-topic. I was tired of feeling like the awkward kid in the room.

And then there were my parents. The "You're lazy" and "Can't you just try harder?" lectures were a broken record. I'd always felt like a misfit, like I could never meet their standards. The ADHD diagnosis made things a little clearer, but it also made me angry. Had they bothered to understand while I was growing up, could things have been different?

I was lost in a fog of self-doubt. Was I really just a screw-up, or was there more to this? I needed to figure it out, and fast.

Social Challenges with ADHD

Deb was not what one would call socially adept. She was a brilliant engineer, quick to solve algorithms and equations. But social cues? They were a foreign language. There she was, at a company dinner, surrounded by colleagues who seemed to effortlessly glide through conversations like ice skaters on a frozen lake. Deb, on the other hand, felt like a penguin trying to learn ballet.

Her attempt at small talk with the CEO went something like this: "So, uh, you know how binary code works? It's really fascinating. I mean, the efficiency of it all…" She trailed off, realizing her enthusiasm for ones and zeros might not be the most riveting dinner conversation.

The CEO, bless his heart, gave her a polite smile and nodded. Deb took that as encouragement and launched into a detailed explanation of the difference between a for loop and a while loop. By the time she finished, the entire table was staring at her, a mixture of confusion and pity in their eyes.

As the evening wore on, Deb managed to accidentally spill red wine on the CFO's white shirt, and then, in a moment of panic, tried to help by rubbing the stain vigorously. Despite the evening's…unique…turn of events, Deb left the dinner with her head held high. After all, she had successfully converted at least one person to the beauty of coding. The CEO, who had politely declined her offer to explain the details of object-oriented programming, now seemed to have a newfound respect for her. Or maybe he was just traumatized. Either way, Deb considered it a win.

Social skills do not come easy for everyone. Especially with ADHD in the mix. One of the biggest challenges is understanding the unspoken codes of social interaction. Things like body language, tone of voice, and those little hints people drop in conversations can be like trying to read a book without knowing the language. Also, ADHD often comes with a tendency to say exactly what's on your mind without thinking about the consequences. This can lead to some pretty awkward moments, and it can damage relationships if it happens too often.

Another common issue is forgetfulness. Remembering names, faces, and even what you talked about last time you saw someone can be a real struggle. It can make people feel unimportant or overlooked, which isn't great for building connections. Then there's the problem of time. ADHD can make it hard to keep track of time, which means you might be late for social events or appointments. This can be frustrating for friends and family, and it can make you feel like you're unreliable.

And let's not forget about the intense focus thing. When you're really into something, it's easy to tune out the world around you. This can make conversations feel one-sided or make you seem disinterested in what other people are saying.

Overthinking is another common issue. After a social interaction, you might replay the conversation in your head, looking for things you could have done differently. This can lead to anxiety and self-doubt.

Maintaining eye contact can be an issue too. It's something that most people do without thinking, but for women with ADHD, it can feel awkward or even impossible.

Feeling different from everyone else can be tough. It's normal to want to fit in, and when you feel like you don't quite belong, it can be lonely.

Having solid social skills goes beyond being popular; it makes your life easier and more fulfilling. First off, your career can really benefit. I'm not just talking about office parties; good social skills affect how you work with others, how you present your ideas, and how you build relationships. Strong social skills can mean the difference between getting that promotion or not.

Beyond work, your personal life will thank you. You get to have deeper connections with your friends and family, resolve conflicts more easily, and feel confident in social situations. And let's not forget about your mental health. Feeling connected to others is like a shield against stress and loneliness. When you have strong social skills, you're better equipped to handle life's ups and downs. So, while it might feel hard at first, working on your social skills is an investment in your overall happiness and success.

Building Stronger Relationships

Relationships are not meant to be perfect. Everyone has quirks that drive their partner crazy. But guess what? Those same quirks are probably what make you amazing in other ways. Your impulsiveness might drive your partner nuts, but it could also be the reason you are so good at problem-solving. So, instead of focusing on the wrongs, you can both work together to appreciate the positive sides of each other's personality.

Not every little thing is worth a fight. Choose your battles; you can't win them all, and some just aren't worth the energy. When you're feeling angry, take a step back. Count to ten, or even take a short break. You'll be amazed at how much calmer you feel. And remember, saying hurtful things in the heat of the moment can damage your relationship.

Relationships work better when you work as a team rather than acting as competitors. It's like being on the same sports team; you win or lose together. Instead of trying to prove who's right, focus on finding a solution that works for both of you. When disagreements happen, try to see things from your partner's perspective. It might not change your mind, but it can help you understand where they're coming from.

It's easy to feel overwhelmed and misunderstood in a relationship, especially when you have ADHD. A little extra patience and understanding can go a long way. Be open and honest (this might sound obvious, but it's a big deal). Talking about your ADHD with people you trust can be a huge relief. It helps them understand you better, and it can also help you feel less alone.

Also, listen more. It might seem counterintuitive, but focusing on what the other person is saying can actually help you connect better. Try to put your thoughts aside for a moment and really listen to what they're saying. You'll be surprised how much closer it brings you. And I know consistency might not come easy, but try your best to be reliable. Show up on time and follow through on your commitments. You can build trust that way.

Lastly, be patient with yourself. Building strong relationships takes time and the ability to compromise. Sometimes you'll need to bend a little to meet someone halfway. Don't get discouraged if things don't go perfectly right away. It takes effort, but it's worth it. Keep trying, and you'll see progress.

Effective Communication Skills

Ever had a conversation that just didn't go as planned? Maybe you felt misunderstood, or maybe the other person seemed completely clueless. Well, there's actually a formula for making sure your message lands. It's called the 7 Cs of Communication, a concept developed by Scott M. Cutlip and Allen H. Center in the 1950s.

First up is *clarity*. Make sure what you're saying is easy to understand. No beating around the bush. Be direct and to the point. Instead of saying, "I'm kind of upset about the situation," try: "I'm really frustrated about how you handled the project."

Next is *conciseness*. Get to the point without rambling on and on. People tend to get distracted when this happens. Instead of saying, "I was thinking maybe we could possibly consider going to the movies sometime soon?", try: "Want to go to the movies this weekend?" Be quick and straight to the point.

Then we've got *concreteness*. Use tangible examples to illustrate your point to help people understand what you're talking about.

Be *correct*. That means be accurate in what you say. Make sure your facts are right and your grammar is on point. Nobody likes to be corrected, so get it right the first time.

Ensure that you are *coherent*. Let what you are saying make sense. Your message should flow smoothly from one point to the next. Instead of jumping from topic to topic, try to stick to one main point at a time.

Completeness means saying everything you need to say. Don't leave out important details. Imagine ordering a pizza and only telling the person to make it with cheese. Not very helpful, right? If you're asking for a favor, be clear about what you need and why. Don't leave out important details.

And finally, we have *courtesy*. Be polite and respectful. Even if you're disagreeing with someone, you can still be nice about it. A little kindness goes a long way.

So, the next time you're having a conversation, keep these 7 Cs in mind. You might be surprised at how much it improves your communication skills.

Social Awareness

At its core, social awareness helps you to connect with the people around you. It's like having a sixth sense for social situations. You are able to "read the room" and respond appropriately. When you're socially aware, you have deeper insight into societal norms and can almost feel the pulse of the community you're part of.

Now, why is this important? Well, being socially aware brings a ton of benefits. For starters, it helps you build positive relationships and communicate more effectively. From a young age, we're naturally inclined to be social, but some people might struggle with this skill. Lacking social awareness can lead to social rejection and isolation.

On the flip side, honing your social awareness can help you understand and connect with others on a deeper level. You'll find yourself better equipped to empathize with people, understand their feelings, and respond in ways that are both kind and effective.

Let me give you some examples. Imagine your friend's dog has just passed away. Being socially aware means you recognize the sadness, grief, and loneliness they might be feeling. You don't make statements like "Stop being so sulky, it's just a dog."

Or let's say your child is throwing a tantrum. Instead of losing your cool, you stay calm, validate their feelings, and respond empathetically. Say your partner comes home after losing their job. Instead of immediately offering solutions or dismissing their concerns, you sit with them, listen attentively, and provide comfort. When it comes to household chores, instead of one person bearing the brunt, you and your partner share responsibilities equally, making it easier for both of you.

If someone has a different political view, being socially aware means you respect their opinion, listen closely, and look for common ground without letting emotions flare up.

So, how do you get better at this? First, develop self-awareness. How you treat yourself is often reflected in how you treat others. You make your beliefs, and then your beliefs make you. When you expand your self-awareness, you can improve your response to various social environments. "Knowing thyself" is the first step toward understanding others.

Next, observe others. Just as you observe yourself, see how people react to your comments and actions. This insight into their emotional states when you socialize will help you know how to relate. Focus on listening actively and carefully to others, and get feedback from those close to you about your social skills.

Practicing forgiveness is another key step. Every thought you think and every word you say forms a blueprint, and your mind must work to make that blueprint real. This principle applies to forgiveness as well. Forgiving others wholeheartedly can improve your quality of life and change your consciousness. It makes you less likely to be overwhelmed by difficult social situations, and improves your ability to deal with people effectively.

Navigating Conflict in Interpersonal Relationships

Interpersonal conflict refers to any type of conflict involving two or more people. It's different from intrapersonal conflict, which refers to an internal conflict within yourself. Whether mild or severe, interpersonal conflict is a natural outcome of human interaction. People have different personalities, values, expectations, and attitudes toward problem-solving. When you work or interact with someone who doesn't share your opinions or goals, a conflict can come up.

Conflict isn't always serious, nor is it always negative. First, you need to figure out the type of conflict. Broadly speaking, conflict happens when two or more people disagree. This disagreement can be verbal, such as an argument, or nonverbal, like someone turning their back or walking away.

The first step in resolving conflict is to figure out what's really going on. Is it a misunderstanding, a difference in opinion, or something deeper? Sometimes, it's helpful to take a step back and look at the situation from the other person's perspective. This can help you see things from their point of view and find common ground.

I spoke about communication earlier. It comes into play here again. Open and honest communication is essential for resolving conflict. Express your feelings and needs clearly, but avoid blaming or accusing the other person. Try to really understand what the other person is saying, without interrupting or getting defensive.

Look for areas of agreement or shared goals. Focusing on commonalities can help you to reduce tension and create a more positive atmosphere. Once you understand the issue and have found some common ground, it's time to brainstorm solutions. Be open to different ideas, and be willing to compromise.

If things get too heated, it's okay to take a break. Step away from the situation and give yourselves time to cool down. This can help prevent things from escalating and allow you to approach the situation with a clearer head. Sometimes, conflict can be too much to handle on your own. You can talk to a mediator or counselor to bring a neutral perspective and help you find a resolution.

Navigating Societal Norms with Neurodiversity

Societal norms are the unwritten rules that guide our behavior in social situations. They influence how we communicate, interact, and see ourselves and others. For neurodivergent minds, these norms can feel restrictive or isolating because they might not match one's natural ways of thinking and behaving. It can feel like you're constantly swimming against the current.

Understanding where these expectations come from and how they make you feel is a great starting point. When you see that these norms aren't personal rules, but societal constructs, you'll get more freedom to be who you are. Surrounding yourself with supportive people is also key. Friends and family who celebrate your individuality can make a world of difference.

Challenging stereotypes can be another powerful way to create change. Whether it's through social media, conversations, or your own actions, you can help shift the narrative by owning your story. You're not defined by expectations or labels. Your worth isn't measured by how well you fit into a mold. Be you.

Also, don't be afraid to question the rules. If something doesn't feel right, speak up. Whether it's a sexist comment or a discriminatory policy, your voice matters. Challenge stereotypes whenever you see them. Be a role model. Inspire others by living your truth. Your actions can challenge stereotypes and create a more inclusive world for future generations.

Setting Boundaries

Setting boundaries might feel counterintuitive. After all, as a woman, you're often expected to be selfless and accommodating. But the thing is, when you constantly put others' needs before your own, you risk feeling overwhelmed, resentful, and depleted. Boundaries are the lines that define your personal space, your values, and your limits. They protect your time, energy, and emotional well-being.

The fact that you have boundaries doesn't mean you're being selfish or uncaring. In fact, it can strengthen your relationships. When you have clear boundaries, you're more present and engaged in the relationships that matter most. You're not distracted by trying to meet everyone else's needs at the expense of your own.

You deserve to be treated with respect. Setting boundaries is a way of communicating that you value yourself and your time, protecting yourself while also teaching others how to treat you. When people know your limits, they're less likely to take advantage of you. It's about self-respect and self-preservation.

The thing is, setting boundaries isn't always easy. There are a number of reasons why you may find it difficult to say no or establish limits. One of the biggest reasons is fear. You worry that people won't like you if you set boundaries. You might fear being seen as selfish or difficult. This fear can be so strong that it overrides your need to look out for yourself.

Some of us are natural-born people pleasers. We want everyone to like us, and we hate to disappoint people. This can lead to overcommitting and neglecting our own needs. If you don't believe you're worthy of your own time and energy, it can be hard to set boundaries. You might feel like you don't deserve to say no.

Difficulty expressing your needs and wants can also make it challenging to set boundaries. You might be afraid of confrontation or coming across as rude. Saying no can feel like missing out on opportunities or fun. Also, if you've always been the caretaker in your relationships, it can be difficult to shift into a mode where you're also taking care of yourself.

Let's deal with the fear of rejection. It's normal to worry about how others will respond when you set a boundary. Challenge these thoughts by reminding yourself that you have the right to say no. People who truly care about you will respect your boundaries.

If you don't believe you deserve good things, challenge these negative thoughts. Everyone deserves to be treated with respect, and that includes you. Yes, you. Saying no can feel awkward or uncomfortable, especially if you're not used to it—so practice assertiveness in low-stakes situations to build confidence. It's easy to get caught up in the idea that you're missing out on something by saying no, but remember, you can't do everything, and it's okay to prioritize your own needs.

Let me give you an example. Your BFF is always calling you to vent about her problems. It's gotten to the point where you feel drained after every conversation. What do you need here? Boundaries. How do you set them? Start by understanding the situation. You care about your friend and want to support her, but you also need to prioritize your own mental health.

You could say something like, "I care about you and I want to be there for you, but I'm feeling overwhelmed right now. I need some time for myself. Can we maybe talk about this again tomorrow?" This approach is assertive without being aggressive. It acknowledges your friend's feelings while also expressing your needs.

Understanding and Managing RSD

(Rejection Sensitive Dysphoria)

Rejection sensitive dysphoria (RSD) is a powerful emotion in response to feeling rejected or criticized, and it's often linked to ADHD. This can take a heavy toll on how you think and on your relationships.

Symptoms of RSD include feeling intense emotional pain if you feel criticized or like you've failed, constantly seeking approval, having low self-esteem, experiencing sudden emotional outbursts, being harsh on yourself, finding it tough to manage relationships, and avoiding social situations.

Everyone has different talents and abilities. Focusing on yours can help boost your self-esteem and counteract the negative feelings that RSD can bring. When you're feeling down about a rejection, remind yourself of your strengths and accomplishments. This builds a fortress of positivity to protect yourself from the emotional storms.

RSD often involves a lot of negative self-talk. When these thoughts creep in, query their validity. Are they based on facts or feelings? Replacing negative thoughts with more positive and realistic ones can make a big difference. And it's okay to feel upset or rejected. Trying to suppress your emotions can make them feel even stronger. Instead, acknowledge your feelings without judgment. This can help you process them more effectively.

Building and Leveraging a Supportive Network

It's not always easy to build and keep relationships when you have ADHD. But having people around you who care can help manage your symptoms and make you feel better overall. There are lots of benefits to having supportive relationships.

Research shows such relationships can help you live healthier and longer. Friends and family can help you deal with stressful times and enjoy the good times more. They can also help you notice when you're feeling stressed or upset, sometimes even before you realize it yourself.

If you want to keep your relationships strong, show your appreciation for such relationships. Stay in touch by calling, texting, or emailing. Be there for your friends when they need you, and accept their help too. Celebrate their successes and be happy for them.

If a friend does something that upsets you, talk about it with them. Try to understand and give them a chance to make things right. Respect your friend's need for space, and if a relationship is draining or negative, maybe it's time to think about whether it still has a place in your support network.

If you're looking to build a robust support system, there are many ways you can meet new people and create meaningful connections. You could volunteer for a cause you care about, join a sports team or gym, start a book club, get to know your neighbors and co-workers, or join professional groups. You can also use social networking sites to stay in touch with friends and family or find support groups for the specific challenges you might be facing.

It's important to build your support system before you need it. Take good care of your current relationships and make new friends now so that when you're going through tough times, you'll have a network to help you through it. Building and using a support network will help you manage your ADHD and improve your overall quality of life.

Understanding Your Partner's Perspective

Every person sees the world differently based on their experiences and beliefs. It's important to respect these differences and understand that neither perspective is right or wrong. ADHD can indeed intensify emotions and make it difficult to regulate them, leading to impulsive reactions or feeling overwhelmed by your partner's point of view.

If this happens, be open to listening. This means concentrating fully on what your partner is saying without planning your response while they are talking. Finding a quiet space, maintaining eye contact, and nodding to show your engagement can help you stay focused while eliminating distractions. Summarizing what your partner has said when they've finished speaking can help you ensure you've understood them correctly. Breaking unproductive patterns, such as interrupting or getting defensive, requires practice. Asking insightful questions, such as about what your partner sees that you might be missing, helps you grasp their perspective.

Once again, you need to prioritize relationships over being right. Show empathy by acknowledging your partner's feelings, even when you don't entirely agree. Additionally, focus on shared relationship goals and finding common ground to strengthen the bond with your partner. This improved understanding can lead to increased intimacy, improved communication, and enhanced emotional support within the relationship. These positive changes not only strengthen the partnership but also aid in developing vital emotional regulation skills to manage ADHD more effectively.

The Role of Trust and Honesty

Trust and honesty are the foundation of a good relationship. Without these, it's hard to feel safe, secure, and connected with your partner. For you, who might already feel misunderstood or judged, having a partner who can be trusted provides crucial stability and support. Trust comes from doing things that are reliable and consistent—whether they're minor things like being on time or big things like being there during tough times. It's important to talk openly about what you can commit to and then follow through on those commitments.

Being truthful goes beyond simply not lying; you need to be transparent and open. Share your thoughts, feelings, and experiences honestly, even when it's hard. Open communication means having some tough conversations.

For you, this might mean talking about how your symptoms affect your behavior and relationships. By being open, truthful, and supportive, you can build a strong, trusting relationship that's based on understanding and respect.

Supporting Each Other's Growth

When two people are evolving and growing, it creates a dynamic and stimulating relationship. It's like having a partner in crime who's constantly leveling up. Supporting each other's dreams and aspirations fosters a deeper emotional bond. It shows that you care about their happiness and fulfillment. When you encourage your partner's growth, you demonstrate respect for their goal and aspirations.

Seeing your partner evolve can inspire you to pursue your own goals, creating a positive and supportive environment for both of you. A partner who feels supported is less likely to harbor resentment or blame. Openly discussing goals and aspirations can also improve communication and understanding.

For example, if your partner is trying to learn a new language, instead of just saying, "Good luck," you could offer to practice with them, or help them find language exchange partners. This shows your partner that you are interested in their growth.

Maybe your partner is incredibly creative but lacks confidence in their abilities. Point out their talents and show them how these strengths can be applied to their goals. Pursuing a goal together can be incredibly bonding as well. You could start a new hobby, take a class, or train for a race together. These shared experiences can bring you closer.

We all have those inner critics that hold us back. Help your partner identify these negative thought patterns and replace them with more positive ones. Be their personal cheerleader, help them overcome self-doubt. The goal is to support your partner's journey, not take over. Encourage independence and celebrate their successes. Your role is to be their biggest fan and their strongest ally.

Worksheet Eight: Relationship Mapping

Step 1: Identify Key Relationships

List the most significant relationships in your life. Consider family, friends, romantic partners, and colleagues.

Relationship Category	Person's Name	Role/Connection
Family		
Friends		
Romantic Partner		
Colleagues		
Others		

Step 2: Assess Relationship Quality

For each person listed, assess the quality of the relationship on a scale of 1 to 5 (1 being poor, 5 being excellent). Provide brief notes on why you rated the relationship as you did.

Person's Name	Quality Rating (1-5)	Notes on Relationship Quality

Step 3: Identify Strengths and Areas for Improvement

Reflect on each relationship and identify its strengths and areas where it could be improved.

Person's Name	Strengths	Areas for Improvement

Step 4: Develop Strategies for Improvement

For each area of improvement identified, develop specific strategies or actions you can take to enhance the relationship.

Person's Name	Area for Improvement	Strategy/Action Plan

Step 5: Implement and Reflect

Implement the strategies you have developed over the next month. Reflect on the changes and note any improvements or challenges.

Person's Name	Strategy Implemented	Outcome/Reflection

Reflection Questions

1. What positive changes have you noticed in your relationships after implementing the strategies?

Answer:

2. What challenges did you encounter while trying to improve your relationships?

Answer:

3. How did you handle these challenges?

Answer:

4. What additional steps can you take to continue improving your interpersonal relationships?

Answer:

5. How have these improvements impacted your overall well-being and emotional regulation?

Answer:

Takeaways

- Recognizing the symptoms and impact of ADHD on relationships is crucial. Educating oneself and one's partner about the condition can foster empathy and pave the way for effective communication and support.

- Open, honest, and respectful communication helps address misunderstandings and frustrations. Regular check-ins and expressing feelings can prevent resentment from building up.

- Balancing responsibilities within the relationship is essential. Acknowledging each partner's strengths and working together to manage tasks can reduce stress and improve harmony.

- Building a relationship that thrives despite ADHD requires patience, compassion, and a commitment to growth. Recognizing that progress may be slow and celebrating small victories can strengthen the bond between partners.

CHAPTER NINE

Leveraging ADHD Strengths

❧

"Success is not final, failure is not fatal: It is the courage to continue that counts."

—Winston Churchill

"And He said to me, 'My grace is sufficient for you, for My strength is made erfect in weakness.' Therefore most gladly I will rather boast in my infirmities, that the power of Christ may rest upon me."

—2 Corinthians 12:9 (NKJV)

Case Study

Nicole sighed deeply as she stepped into her workplace. She was just plain tired. Another day, another battle with her overactive mind. Her colleagues, with their measured tones and organized desks, were a stark contrast to her chaotic world. A simple question and she was already on the defensive, leaving her coworkers exchanging bewildered glances. She knew she was too loud, too enthusiastic, but dialing it back felt like trying to tame a hurricane.

Mr. Thompson, her boss, was a different kind of challenge. His world was black and white, efficiency and deadlines. Nicole's work habits clashed violently with his structured approach. Her ideas, often brilliant but scattered, were met with skepticism rather than encouragement. She constantly felt like she was just one misstep away from being labeled as incompetent.

Disclosing ADHD at Work

ADHD comes with challenges, but also strengths that can help you at work. Traits like quickly coming up with ideas, being able to concentrate on the task at hand, and thinking creatively are very useful in the workplace. I need you to see these as special abilities that you can harness to improve your work output. Singer/songwriter Solange Knowles once confessed that her ADHD diagnosis drastically influences her creative process. This shows that understanding and valuing these traits can change how you approach your work and how others see you. Who says ADHD cannot be to your advantage?

For instance, the tendency to get easily distracted is actually a sign of your adaptability and quick thinking. It might mean you notice details that others miss. Impulsivity could be seen as a talent for making quick decisions. Michelle Rodriguez, known for her role in the *Fast & Furious* franchise and other major films, claims that her impulsiveness and high energy have helped her take on diverse projects, maintaining a dynamic and successful career. When you change your perception of these traits, you can show their value and use them to your advantage at work.

I need you to know that deciding whether to tell your employer about your ADHD is a personal choice. It has advantages and disadvantages. Let's examine these, and then it's up to you to make the choice you deem most suitable for you.

Benefits of telling your employer:

- You can ask for specific help to do your job better. For example, you could ask for a quieter place to work, more flexible hours, or the chance to work from home some of the time.

- It can lead to more open and honest talk. You can talk about what you're good at and what's hard for you, making it easier to find ways to maximize your strengths and compensate for your weaknesses.

- Lastly, and quite importantly, it will help in the campaign to create a more suitable workplace culture for others like you. The more employers are adjusted to the realities of working with people with ADHD or neurodiversity, the more they'll be compelled to adapt their work culture to suit your needs. If you tell them, it can help your coworkers and managers understand and support both you and others.

Now that we've discussed the advantages, it's also good to look at the disadvantages.

- Unfortunately, some employers or colleagues might have biases or misunderstandings about ADHD, which could affect their perception of your abilities and impact job opportunities or performance evaluations.

- There is a risk of being treated differently, either negatively or overly helpful, which can feel patronizing.

- Lastly, it would mean you have to share personal information, and I know not too many people are comfortable with doing that.

Before discussing your ADHD at work, you need to have adequately researched and understand the accommodations you need and be prepared to discuss them specifically with your employer. When talking about it, you should focus on your strengths and how the accommodations will help you excel in your role.

It's also important to be aware of your legal rights regarding workplace accommodations and anti-discrimination laws. This will help you know what to accept and what not to take.

Seeking Accommodations at Work for ADHD

There are ways to make your work environment more supportive and set you up for success. The Americans with Disabilities Act (ADA) makes sure that employees with ADHD can get reasonable accommodations to help them do their jobs effectively.

To get these accommodations, you need to first assess your needs. How is your job affected by your ADHD? Do you find it difficult to concentrate during long meetings? Do you struggle with staying organized or managing your time effectively?

Once you do this, you also have to decide what you share. I would advise that you focus more on how ADHD directly affects your work. When talking about your ADHD, keep the conversation professional. Discuss the specific challenges you face and how they affect your job performance. For example, you might say, "I have trouble focusing during long meetings, which sometimes causes me to miss details and affects my ability to meet deadlines."

You can discuss this with your boss, a supervisor, or your HR department. If you're uncertain about talking to your boss, reaching out to HR first might feel more comfortable. Once you know what accommodations you need, ask your employer for them. If you decide to talk to HR, they can help you with the process and keep your request private.

Under the ADA, employers must provide accommodations unless it causes significant difficulty or expense. Reasonable accommodations for ADHD include time off for therapy sessions, flexible deadlines for non-urgent projects, the use of noise-canceling headphones, providing structured tasks, and access to a quiet room if working in an open-plan office.

Employers with 15 or more workers must give these accommodations by law. If you experience unfair treatment or if your employer denies reasonable accommodations, you have the right to get legal help or file a complaint with the Equal Employment Opportunity Commission (EEOC).

Managing Workplace Relationships and Dynamics

Workplace relationships can make or break your job experience. Strong connections with colleagues boosts morale, increases productivity, and even leads to career growth. On the other hand, poor relationships can create a stressful work environment and hinder your success. When people get along, they're more likely to collaborate, share ideas, and support each other.

How can you build and maintain positive relationships? Start by being a good communicator. Be clear, honest, and respectful. Active listening is key. Show your colleagues that you value their input by paying attention to what they say. Trust is another important factor. Be reliable, keep your promises, and be transparent.

Conflict is inevitable in any workplace, but how you handle it matters. Address issues directly and calmly. Focus on finding solutions rather than placing blame. And remember, it's okay to talk to your supervisor or HR if you're struggling to resolve a conflict on your own.

Let's talk about the less fun side of office life: dealing with difficult coworkers. These people can range from the overly dramatic to the downright rude. But don't worry, there are ways to handle them without losing your cool.

Start by understanding the problem. Is it constant complaining, taking credit for your work, or something else? How is this behavior affecting your work and mood? Is there a reason for their behavior? Are they stressed, overworked, or just having a bad day?

Once you understand what the problem is, take action. If possible, have a calm and private conversation with the coworker. Clearly explain how their behavior is affecting you. Let them know what you will and won't tolerate. Be assertive but respectful. Keep a record of incidents if the problem persists. This can be helpful if you need to involve HR. If direct communication doesn't work, try to minimize your interactions with them.

Leveraging ADHD Strengths in Career and Professional Growth

Reframing common ADHD traits as positive attributes can really change your perspective and boost your confidence. For example, being easily distracted can be seen as the ability to multitask and switch between tasks quickly, which can be helpful in fast-moving work environments. Impulsiveness can be seen as making quick decisions and thinking on your feet, which is helpful in situations that need fast responses and creative solutions. Hyperfocus can lead to high productivity and deep engagement with tasks, making it valuable when working on complex projects.

In the workplace, you can use the creativity that often comes with ADHD to your advantage in brainstorming sessions and when solving problems. You can also make use of your ability to hyperfocus and generate ideas quickly in roles that call for constant innovation and fresh perspectives. We all want to be upward mobile in our careers, and your ADHD doesn't have to be the anchor that drags you down the drain—instead, it can be leverage that catapults you to achieve great success in all that you do.

In fact, nothing is stopping you from owning your own business. Starting and running a business can be an excellent fit for women with ADHD. The entrepreneurial path gives you the flexibility to create a work environment tailored to your needs and strengths.

Sara Blakely, founder of Spanx, turned a $5,000 investment into a billion-dollar company by revolutionizing the shapewear industry. She is recognized as one of the most influential women entrepreneurs. Her impulsiveness and ability to think outside the box helped her come up with the idea for Spanx and take bold steps to market her product. She had some failures along the way, but she learned to rebound like a pro.

You can be like her by recognizing and affirming positive outcomes of your efforts, which can counterbalance the natural tendency to dwell on negatives.

Remember, perfectionism can be paralyzing. Instead of being fixated on "perfect," adapt the concept of "messy action"—that is, get started on projects and tasks even when everything isn't perfectly lined up. This helps you move forward and make progress. Focus on simplifying and streamlining your processes, such as using templates for repetitive tasks, batching similar activities together, and using visual planners to keep track of your to-do lists. This minimizes overwhelm and helps you stay organized.

Hyperfocus can also be channeled correctly. Find a quiet space free from interruptions. Ensure you have everything you need within reach. Dedicate specific time blocks to tasks that demand intense focus. This way, you can use your hyperfocus to deal with more difficult assignments or learn something new.

Simplicity is key. Avoid overcomplicating your business operations and focus on essential tasks. Eliminating unnecessary complexities helps maintain clarity and reduces cognitive load, making it easier to manage your responsibilities effectively.

Worksheet: Navigating Challenges in the Workplace

List at least five common challenges you face or have observed in the workplace. Think about various aspects such as interpersonal relationships, workload, resources, and work-life balance.

1._____

2._____

3._____

4._____

5._____

Choose two challenges from the list above and provide a brief explanation of why these challenges occur and how they impact your work.

Challenge 1:

- Description:

_____

_____

_____

_____

- Why it occurs:

_____

_____

_____

_____

- Impact on work:

_____

_____

_____

_____

Challenge 2:

- Description:

_____

_____

_____

_____

_____

- Why it occurs:

_____

_____

_____

_____

- Impact on work:

_____

_____

_____

_____

For each of the challenges described above, list at least three strategies you could use to manage or overcome them effectively.

Challenge 1:

- Strategy 1:

- Strategy 2:

- Strategy 3:

Challenge 2:

- Strategy 1:

- Strategy 2:

- Strategy 3:

Create a personal action plan to improve your ability to handle workplace challenges. Set specific, achievable goals, and outline the steps you will take to reach these goals.

Action Plan:

- Goal 1:

    - Steps to Achieve:

        1. _____
        2. _____
        3. _____

- **Goal 2:**

  ▪ Steps to Achieve:

    1. _____
    2. _____
    3. _____

Takeaways

  ▪ Recognize that qualities often seen as challenges, such as hyperfocus, creativity, and spontaneity, can be powerful assets when properly harnessed and directed.

  ▪ Tailor your approach to productivity and organization to fit your unique mind. Techniques like using visual aids, breaking tasks into smaller steps, and leveraging technology can help you manage ADHD effectively.

  ▪ Understand that your divergent mind brings a unique perspective and skillset that can offer innovative solutions and fresh insights in various aspects of life and work.

  ▪ Surround yourself with people who understand and appreciate your strengths and challenges. Seek out communities and resources that give you support and validation for your experiences.

CHAPTER TEN

Long-Term Wellness

✦

"It's not selfish to love yourself, take care of yourself, and to make your happiness a priority. It's necessary."

—Mandy Hale

"But those who wait on the Lord Shall renew their strength; They shall mount up with wings like eagles, They shall run and not be weary, They shall walk and not faint."

—Isaiah 40:31 (NKJV)

Case Study

Jane, a 32-year-old graphic designer, was diagnosed with ADHD just two years ago. For most of her life, she felt like she was barely keeping her head above water—constantly overwhelmed, struggling to keep up with work, and feeling misunderstood by friends and family. Emotional regulation was a huge challenge for her. Even minor frustrations could lead to explosive outbursts or days of deep sadness, leaving her drained and isolated.

Jane's struggles weren't just emotional. She found it challenging to maintain relationships, often feeling guilty for snapping at loved ones or withdrawing when things got too intense. At work, she feared being seen as unreliable because of her occasional bouts of hyperfocus, followed by days where she could hardly get anything done. The diagnosis of ADHD brought some clarity, but it also left her feeling even more frustrated. "Why can't I just control my emotions like everyone else?" she often wondered.

Integrating Routine Physical Activity for Cognitive Benefits

Exercise is really good for your brain. Regular physical activity has been linked to improved memory, attention, problem-solving skills, and overall brain health. It stimulates the growth of new brain cells, increases blood flow to the brain, and reduces stress hormones that can impair cognitive function.

I know that finding time for exercise can be a little difficult, but even small amounts can make a difference. You can start with short workouts and gradually increase duration and intensity. Then, find activities that you enjoy. This will make it easier to stick to your exercise routine.

Nothing's stopping you from making it social. Exercise with friends or join a fitness class for added motivation. You could dance as a fun way to improve memory, coordination, and rhythm. And break it up; if you can't find a large block of time, try short periods of activity throughout the day.

Aerobic exercise like running, swimming, or cycling increases heart rate and oxygen flow to the brain. Building muscle can improve cognitive function and reduce the risk of age-related decline.

Plan for at least 150 minutes of moderate-intensity exercise or 75 minutes of vigorous-intensity exercise per week. Even small amounts of physical activity can have a positive impact on your brain health.

By making exercise part of your routine, you can help your brain stay sharp and healthy for a long time. It can protect against diseases like

Alzheimer's and Parkinson's, reduce the chance of memory problems, delay dementia, and improve brain structure.

The Importance of Self-Care

Self-care is important for staying healthy and happy. It involves taking deliberate actions to nurture your body, mind, and spirit and requires being mindful and intentional about your needs. There are many things you can gain from self-care, including stress management, improved physical and mental health, better relationships, and a clearer mind and calmer demeanor.

Regular self-care activities such as exercise, healthy eating, and adequate sleep directly impact physical health, strengthening the body and boosting the immune system. Taking care of yourself also enables you to be more present and engaged in relationships, enhancing communication skills and making it easier to set healthy boundaries.

Incorporating self-care into daily routines can be simple. It can involve small, manageable actions, such as a short walk or meditation each day. Treat self-care like any other obligation by scheduling specific times for activities that nourish you. Pay attention to your body and mind and prioritize rest or relaxation when needed. Shifting your focus to the positive aspects of your life through gratitude practices and seeking support from friends, family, or a therapist are also important aspects of self-care. When you incorporate self-care into your daily routine, you're not only taking care of yourself but also laying the groundwork for a happier, more fulfilling life. You can't pour from an empty cup— so take the time to fill yours up.

Your Self-Care Routine

Creating a self-care routine is essential for taking care of yourself and staying balanced and happy. Whether you're just starting out or want to improve what you're already doing, there are many ways to create a self-care routine that works for you. The basis involves treating yourself with kindness, changing your inner conversations, and developing a nurturing routine. Setting boundaries, learning to say no, decluttering where you live and work, and spending time outside are also crucial for a good self-care routine.

A spa day is the ultimate indulgence. You can go for a massage. Relax your muscles and soothe your mind with a Swedish, deep tissue, or hot stone massage. Don't forget facials also. Treat your skin to a deep cleanse, exfoliation, and hydration. Exfoliate your skin with a body scrub and leave it feeling refreshed and renewed. Saunas and steam rooms help to detoxify your body and relax your muscles.

Healthy hair is a crown you should wear proudly. Go for regular trims to prevent split ends and maintain hair health. Nourish your hair with deep conditioning treatments, and reduce damage and breakage with styles like braids or buns.

A glowing complexion starts with good skincare. Remove dirt and impurities with a gentle cleanser. Keep your skin hydrated with a suitable moisturizer. Protect your skin from harmful UV rays.

Can't afford a vacation for your mental health? Try a staycation. Simply curl up on your sofa with a nice bowl of popcorn and some good Netflix. The goal is to spend some time with yourself and away from the routine.

Nutrition and ADHD

Did you know that managing ADHD isn't just about medication and therapy? Nutrition actually plays a significant role in controlling ADHD symptoms. It's wild how specific diets can either help or worsen the symptoms. For example, diets high in processed foods and sugars can make ADHD symptoms worse, while diets rich in whole foods, like fruits, veggies, lean proteins, and healthy fats, can actually improve symptoms.

Fueling Your Brain for Focus and Balance

While it's not a cure-all, a balanced diet helps to improve focus, attention, and overall well-being. Foods rich in complex carbohydrates and protein release energy gradually, helping to prevent the energy crashes and mood swings often associated with ADHD. Below, I've listed a few good options to include in your meals.

Omega-3 fatty acids are good for brain health and can help improve your focus and attention. They're found in fatty fish like salmon, flaxseeds, chia seeds, and walnuts.

Protein helps stabilize blood sugar levels, preventing energy crashes and mood swings. Good sources include lean meats, poultry, eggs, beans, and lentils.

Complex carbohydrates provide sustained energy without causing blood sugar spikes. Opt for whole grains like brown rice, quinoa, and whole-wheat bread. Don't forget your fruits and vegetables. They are packed with vitamins, minerals, and antioxidants and support overall brain health.

Try to avoid processed foods and sugary drinks. These can cause energy crashes and mood swings. Studies have also shown that there's a link between artificial additives / color and hyperactivity.

A food timetable can also help. To create one, observe your hunger cues. When do you typically feel hungry? Check your energy levels. When do you experience energy slumps or crashes? Also, consider your work schedule. When do you have breaks for meals?

Once you do this, set regular meal times. Aim for three main meals per day: breakfast, lunch, and dinner. You can also plan for two or three healthy snacks between meals. And if you find that you're too busy to cook, prepare meals in advance to save time. Have healthy snacks ready to go. If you live with others, create a family meal plan.

Here's a sample food timetable. You can tweak it to create something that works for you.

7:00 AM: Breakfast (e.g., oatmeal with berries and nuts)

10:00 AM: Snack (e.g., Greek yogurt with honey)

12:00 PM: Lunch (e.g., salad with grilled chicken)

3:00 PM: Snack (e.g., apple slices with peanut butter)

6:00 PM: Dinner (e.g., salmon with roasted vegetables)

Prioritizing Your Mental Health

Taking care of your mental health is like tending to a garden: it needs regular attention and care to thrive. It's an ongoing process that requires dedication and awareness. There are simple yet effective ways to prioritize your mental health. When you feel good mentally, you're better equipped to connect with others on a deeper level.

A clear and focused mind leads to better performance at work. Strong mental health helps you bounce back from challenges. Your mental and physical health are interconnected; one often affects the other. So as much as I encourage you to take care of your physical health, you also need to prioritize your mental health.

Starting a gratitude journal can help reframe your mindset, training your mind to notice and appreciate the positives, thus serving as a buffer against stress and negativity.

Again, you need to learn to say a strong NO. Protecting your mental and emotional energy by declining additional commitments when needed is not selfish.

Finding a form of movement that feels good for you can help reduce stress and anxiety while also improving your mood.

Scheduling personal time for yourself, even if it's just a few minutes each day, can make a significant difference in maintaining balance and preventing burnout.

Creating a relaxing bedtime routine, such as turning off screens an hour before bed and practicing relaxation techniques, will help you wind down for a restful sleep. (Aim for 7 hours per night.)

Eating a balanced diet with regular meals, staying hydrated, and being mindful of alcohol and caffeine intake can significantly impact how you feel.

Developing a routine and finding ways to get organized can bring a sense of order and stability to your life, helping reduce stress and create a clearer mind.

Lastly, find joy and practice self-compassion. Get involved in things that bring you happiness, surround yourself with supportive people, and speak to yourself with kindness. It's important to remember that taking care of yourself is not just okay—it's essential.

Sleep Hygiene Practices for Better Rest

Getting a good night's sleep can sometimes be challenging, but it doesn't have to be. The key to better rest lies in something called "sleep hygiene," which means having habits and behaviors that promote good sleep quality. Here are some simple but effective sleep hygiene practices to help you get the sleep you need.

First, try to go to bed and wake up at the same time every day to help your body get used to a routine. Make your bedroom a good place to sleep by keeping it cool, dark, and quiet and by using curtains to block out light. Also, try to limit your screen time before bed by avoiding phones, tablets, and computers, as the light they emit can make it hard to sleep.

Be mindful of what you eat and drink, as these can affect your sleep quality. Avoid caffeine in the afternoon and evening, and don't eat heavy meals or drink alcohol close to bedtime. Spend time outdoors and exercise during the day, and establish a calming routine before bed to help you relax. Use your bed only for sleep and intimacy, not for working or watching TV. If you need to nap, keep it short and try to nap earlier in the day so it doesn't interfere with your nighttime sleep.

Managing stress and anxiety is essential for better sleep, and if you can't sleep, it's better to get out of bed and do something relaxing until you feel sleepy again. Good sleep hygiene is essential for your overall health and well-being. Consistent, quality sleep can improve your mood, cognitive function, and physical health and reduce the risk of developing chronic conditions like heart disease, diabetes, and mental health disorders. By practicing these sleep hygiene tips, you can set yourself up for better sleep and, as a result, better days ahead. Start with one or two of these tips and see how they impact your sleep—you might be surprised at how much better you feel.

Stress Management Techniques That Work for ADHD

Managing stress is so important, especially for women dealing with ADHD. It can make symptoms worse and create a cycle where stress worsens ADHD and vice versa. But you know what? There are some efficient ways to break this cycle and manage stress while dealing with ADHD.

First off, we've already thoroughly covered the fact that regular exercise, getting enough sleep, and being mindful of what you eat is vital. Meditation can also really help calm the mind and reduce impulsivity, even if you start with a few minutes a day.

Then there's identifying and managing stress triggers, like disorganization or time management challenges. Building a solid support network and incorporating relaxation techniques into your daily routine can also help. And remember, sticking to your treatment plan, learning to advocate for yourself, and being kind to yourself are all super important, too.

By incorporating these strategies into your daily life, you can manage stress more effectively and create a balanced, fulfilling life that celebrates your experiences with ADHD.

Finding Joy

It's so easy to get caught up in all the stuff we have to do every day, and we end up with no time for the things that make us happy. But finding time for hobbies isn't just a nice-to-have; it's essential for our mental and emotional well-being. Hobbies help us deal with stress and give us a mental break from all the everyday pressures. Whether it's painting, gardening, or solving puzzles, doing something you enjoy helps you shift your focus and feel refreshed.

Having hobbies also makes us feel good about ourselves and more confident. Learning something new or getting better at something we love can make all the other challenges in life seem more straightforward to handle. Hobbies also help us make connections with other people and reduce feelings of loneliness. They make life feel more meaningful and exciting. Whether it's stimulating your mind, staying active, or both, hobbies keep you sharp and feeling good overall.

To find or rediscover your hobbies, think about what you enjoy and try new things. Reconnecting with old hobbies can bring back happy memories, and experimenting with new activities might lead you to something you really love. Making time for fun doesn't have to take up a lot of time—just spending 15 minutes a day doing something you enjoy can become a habit that adds balance and joy to your life. Just enjoy the process, and don't worry about being perfect. Hobbies aren't about being perfect; they're about having fun and enjoying yourself as you go.

Hobbies give you a way to be creative, relieve stress, and feel happy and fulfilled. When you really get into doing something you love, it can feel almost like meditation, where you forget about all your worries and focus on the present. So, hobbies aren't just something to do in your free time; they're essential for living a happy, balanced life. When you find and keep doing things that make you happy, you're taking care of yourself and making your life feel more prosperous, more meaningful, and deeply satisfying.

Dealing With Setbacks

Dealing with challenges is a normal part of life, especially if you have ADHD. However, setbacks can be opportunities for growth and learning if you approach them with the right mindset and strategies. It's essential to see setbacks as chances to learn rather than failures and to treat yourself with kindness and understanding. Reflecting on setbacks and learning from them can help you understand your strengths and areas for growth.

To deal with setbacks effectively, surround yourself with people who understand and encourage you, as this can help you see things from a different perspective and find solutions. Celebrating small wins, acknowledging your progress, and staying persistent is essential in dealing with setbacks and building resilience and confidence.

Another helpful strategy is to regularly review your progress, identify areas where you can improve, and make necessary adjustments. By reframing setbacks as opportunities for growth, being kind to yourself, learning from experiences, and maintaining a positive mindset and persistence, you can face setbacks with confidence. Setbacks are a normal part of life, but with the right approach, they don't have to hold you back.

Living a Life That Celebrates Your Neurodiversity

Let me emphasize this: Living a life that celebrates neurodiversity involves embracing the unique ways your brain works, recognizing your strengths, and using them to your advantage. Conditions like ADHD, autism, dyslexia, and more bring their own set of challenges and gifts. Embracing your unique strengths is crucial. As a woman with ADHD, you might have incredible creativity, out-of-the-box thinking, and the ability to hyperfocus on tasks that excite you. By focusing on what you're naturally good at and reframing challenges as opportunities for growth, you can build a life that not only accommodates your neurodivergent mind but thrives because of it.

Advocating for yourself is crucial. This means speaking up about your needs, whether it's asking for accommodations at work, explaining your neurodivergence to friends and family, or seeking support in your personal life. Surrounding yourself with understanding and appreciative people can provide encouragement, valuable insights, and a sense of belonging. Additionally, taking care of your mental health is vital, especially when navigating the challenges of neurodiversity. Incorporating self-care practices as discussed in a previous section can help you maintain a positive outlook on life.

Neurodiversity is a journey of self-discovery and ongoing learning. It's essential to stay curious and open to new strategies, tools, and resources.

This might include learning more about your specific condition, exploring different therapeutic approaches, or connecting with others who share similar experiences. Finally, acknowledging and celebrating your achievements helps you appreciate how far you've come, especially on tough days. By embracing who you are, advocating for your needs, and surrounding yourself with support, you can build a vibrant, fulfilling life that celebrates neurodiversity.

The Role of Professional Therapy in Ongoing Treatment

Professional therapy is essential for treating ADHD. It offers tools and support to enhance quality of life. Therapy can help you manage emotions through skills like mindfulness and distress tolerance, improve your relationships, and give you skills for practical life management. This includes developing communication skills, setting boundaries, and managing daily tasks. Additionally, therapy addresses co-occurring conditions like anxiety and depression. Most importantly, it empowers individuals to become advocates for themselves and helps them set and achieve meaningful long-term goals.

Worksheet: Your Self-Care Plan

Step 1: Identify Your Self-Care Needs

Start by reflecting on the different areas of your life that require attention. Think about what makes you feel balanced, energized, and supported.

Instructions:

Check all the areas that you feel need more attention:

- Physical Health: Exercise, sleep, nutrition
- Emotional Well-being: Managing stress, practicing self-compassion
- Mental Stimulation: Learning, creativity, hobbies
- Social Connections: Relationships, support networks
- Spiritual Growth: Meditation, connecting with nature
- Professional Life: Work-life balance, career satisfaction
- Personal Growth: Goals, aspirations, personal development

Step 2: Create Your Self-Care Menu

Think of this as a menu of activities you can choose from to meet your self-care needs. The idea is to have a variety of options that you can pick from depending on your mood, energy level, and available time.

Instructions:

For each area you checked in Step 1, list 3-5 activities you enjoy or find beneficial. Be specific and realistic.

Example:

- Physical Health
  - Morning journaling (10 minutes)
  - Take a walk in the park (20 minutes)
  - Drink a green smoothie
- Emotional Well-being
  - Practice deep breathing exercises (5 minutes)

- Journal my thoughts and feelings (10 minutes)
- Listen to calming music

Your Menu:

Physical Health

    1._____

    2._____

    3._____

Emotional Well-being

    1._____

    2._____

    3._____

Mental Stimulation

    1._____

    2._____

    3._____

Social Connections

    1._____

    2._____

    3._____

Spiritual Growth

    1._____

2._____

3._____

Professional Life

1._____

2._____

3._____

Personal Growth

1._____

2._____

3._____

Step 3: Schedule Your Self-Care Time

Now that you have your self-care menu, it's time to make self-care a regular part of your routine. Scheduling helps ensure you prioritize your well-being.

Instructions:

Choose at least one activity from your menu and schedule it into your week. You can start small, but consistency is more important than duration.

Example:

- Monday: Journaling (10 minutes) at 7:00 AM
- Wednesday: Call a friend (15 minutes) at 6:00 PM

- Friday: Read a chapter of a book (20 minutes) at 8:00 PM

Your Schedule:

Day: _____   Activity: _____

Time: _____

Day: _____   Activity: _____

Time: _____

Day: _____   Activity: _____

Time: _____

_____

Step 4: Reflect and Adjust

Self-care is a dynamic process. What works one week might need adjustment the next. Reflect on how your self-care plan is working for you.

Instructions:

At the end of each week, take a few minutes to reflect on your self-care activities. What felt good? What was challenging? What adjustments can you make?

Reflection Questions:

- Which activities made the biggest positive impact on my well-being?

- Were there any barriers to completing my self-care activities? If so, what were they?

- What changes can I make to better meet my self-care needs next week?

Your Reflections:

Wins: _____

Challenges: _____

Adjustments: _____

Step 5: Make a Commitment

Finally, commit to your self-care plan. Remember, self-care isn't selfish—it's essential for your overall well-being.

Instructions:

Write a short commitment statement to yourself.

Example:

"I commit to prioritizing my self-care because I deserve to feel balanced, energized, and supported. I will take small, consistent steps each week to nurture my well-being."

Your Commitment:

_____

_____

_____

Takeaways

- Developing and maintaining consistent self-care practices is important for long-term wellness. It helps manage the unique challenges of ADHD, reduces stress, and supports emotional balance.

- Learn to effectively communicate your needs and boundaries. By advocating for yourself, you empower yourself to create environments that support your well-being and productivity.

- Recognize the strengths that come with ADHD and leverage them in personal and professional settings.

- Future planning isn't just about setting goals—you need to build resilience and adapt strategies that align with your values and aspirations. This includes setting realistic, achievable milestones that reflect your long-term vision.

Before You Turn the Page...

Dear Reader,

I hope you're enjoying this book as much as I enjoyed writing it. If the ideas and stories within these pages have resonated with you, inspired you, or simply provided a few moments of escape, I'd be honored if you'd share your thoughts with others.

Leaving a review on Amazon takes just a few seconds, but it can make a world of difference. Your feedback not only supports my work but also guides other readers in discovering books they'll truly connect with.

Option 1: Click the link below and let the world know what you think!

>> Leave a review on Amazon US <<

>> Leave a review on Amazon UK <<

Option 2: Scan the QR code below with your phone's camera to go directly to the review page.

<u>>> Leave a review on Amazon US <<</u>

<u>>> Leave a review on Amazon UK <<</u>

Thank you for taking the time to read this book, and thank you in advance for sharing your experience with the world.

Happy reading!

Now, on to the final chapter…

CHAPTER ELEVEN

Empowerment and Personal Growth

"Courage doesn't always roar. Sometimes courage is the quiet voice at the end of the day saying, 'I will try again tomorrow.'"

—Mary Anne Radmacher

"For I know the thoughts that I think toward you, says the Lord, thoughts of peace and not of evil, to give you a future and a hope."

—Jeremiah 29:11 (NKJV)

Case Study

Fiona sat at a small table in a cozy coffee shop, the aroma of freshly brewed coffee wafting through the air. As she stirred her cup absentmindedly, her mind drifted to the countless therapy sessions she had attended over the years. Each one felt like a dead end, leaving her more frustrated than before. She had never quite found the support she was seeking.

Her thoughts were interrupted when Janet and Jessica joined her, their faces mirroring the exhaustion she felt. As they settled into their seats, Fiona opened up about her experience. *"I've been bouncing from one therapist to another for years,"* she admitted with a sigh. *"It feels like no one really* understands me. I try so hard to explain what's going on in my head, but they just don't get it."

Janet nodded in agreement, her expression one of empathy. "I hear you. It's like we have to educate them about our own struggles. I spent years not even knowing I had ADHD. I just thought I was bad at life, failing at everything I tried. It took so long to find someone who saw past the surface and actually listened to what I was saying."

Jessica, who had been quietly sipping her coffee, leaned in with a knowing look. "Same here," she said. "I didn't get diagnosed until I was 30, and that was only because I finally found a psychiatrist who asked the right questions. Before that, it was like I was just another face in the crowd to them."

The frustration in Fiona's voice was palpable as she recounted her own journey. "Exactly! I went through at least 10 different professionals before someone even mentioned ADHD. It's so frustrating, especially when you're trying so hard to advocate for yourself. I'd walk into those offices, armed with research, trying to explain how I felt, but it was like they weren't even listening."

Janet sighed deeply, the weight of her experiences clear in her tone. "And it's not just the ADHD. I feel like there's this whole other layer because I'm a woman. Most of the research is on boys, so we get missed or misdiagnosed. I kept being told I was just anxious or that I needed to 'try harder' to focus. No one ever thought to check if there was something deeper going on."

Jessica's thoughts turned to her own background as she added, "Yeah, and when you add in cultural stuff, it gets even more complicated. I come from a community where mental health isn't really talked about, and finding someone who understands that makes it even harder. I've had therapists who didn't get why certain things mattered to me or why I was afraid to even bring up the idea of ADHD with my family."

Fiona nodded in agreement, a look of shared understanding passing between them. "Oh, I get that. I've had similar experiences. It's like, we're already struggling with our own minds, and then we have to deal with people who don't get the full picture. It's exhausting."

Janet leaned back in her chair, a thoughtful expression on her face. "I know, right? And it's like, how long do we have to keep fighting to get someone to listen? It's not like we're asking for much, just to be understood and to get the help we need."

Despite the heaviness of the conversation, Jessica smiled softly, her voice carrying a note of optimism. "But hey, at least we're figuring it out now. I mean, it sucks that it took this long, but we're finally getting somewhere, right?"

Fiona returned her smile, feeling a sense of camaraderie with these women who understood her struggles so well. "Yeah, you're right. It's still a battle, but I'm glad we're not fighting it alone anymore. And now, we can help other women avoid going through what we did."

Janet raised her cup in a toast, her smile growing as she looked at her friends. "Here's to finally being seen and heard and to making sure the next generation doesn't have to wait as long as we did."

Jessica clinked her cup with theirs, a sense of hope filling the air between them. "Cheers to that!"

As the three women continued their conversation, there was a sense of solidarity and understanding that had been missing from their previous experiences. They knew the road ahead wouldn't be easy, but together, they felt stronger and more capable of navigating it. And with that shared strength, they were ready to face whatever came next.

Setting Goals with ADHD: A DBT-Informed Approach

Some of the challenges you'll face if you've been diagnosed with ADHD are how to manage your time, start tasks, and prioritize effectively. The good news is that the therapeutic approach called dialectical behavior therapy (DBT) can greatly assist you in making goal-setting more manageable. DBT emphasizes the importance of mindfulness, handling setbacks, and managing emotions, which can ultimately help you to set realistic goals and maintain motivation.

In addition to DBT, utilizing the SMART framework can also be beneficial. This involves setting goals that are Specific, Measurable, Achievable, Relevant, and Time-based. You need to break down long-term goals into smaller, more manageable steps, each with its own deadlines.

It's absolutely okay to adjust your plans if something isn't working as expected. Being flexible is essential. By integrating DBT techniques with SMART goal-setting strategies that are compatible with ADHD, it's possible to bolster your motivation and stay focused on reaching your objectives.

The Importance of Advocacy: A Key to Thriving with ADHD

Advocating for yourself, especially when you're a woman with ADHD, is so important. Unfortunately, many are literally too scared to do that. It's actually simple. All you need to do is speak up for your needs and make sure people around you understand and respect them. When you do that, it totally changes your life, both personally and professionally.

Self-advocacy might feel overwhelming at first, especially when you've just been diagnosed with ADHD, but it's totally worth it. It helps you understand your strengths and challenges, communicate your needs effectively (leading to healthier relationships and a more supportive environment), and ask for the support you need in different parts of your life.

If you want to be an effective advocate, there are some practical tips to keep in mind. You've got to know your worth, communicate your needs clearly and specifically, be assertive without being aggressive, seek support when you need it, and be patient and persistent as you develop this skill.

In the end, self-advocacy is like a lifeline. It allows you to make sure your voice is heard, your needs are met, and you're living authentically. It helps you navigate challenges, build stronger connections, and ultimately find more fulfillment in your life.

Legal Protections and Accommodations for ADHD in the Workplace

Working with ADHD can be tough, but there are laws out there to support you. Have you ever heard of the Americans with Disabilities Act (ADA)? It stops any kind of unfair treatment against people with disabilities, including ADHD. If your ADHD makes it tough to do really important things in your life, then the ADA has your back. If your workplace has 15 or more employees, they need to make changes to help you do your job well, whether that's finding you a quiet place to work, setting flexible hours, providing written instructions, or even adjusting some of your job duties.

So, let's talk about whether or not you need to tell your boss about your ADHD. According to the ADA, you only need to let them know if you want help with your ADHD at work, but you're not forced to tell them during the hiring process or at any specific time. It's totally up to you. It might actually be a good idea to give them a note from your doctor to confirm your diagnosis and the types of help you need. Now, if you feel like your rights under the ADA are being ignored, you should first talk to your supervisor or HR. If that doesn't help, you've got the option to make a complaint to the U.S. Equal Employment Opportunity Commission (EEOC). If the EEOC doesn't help, you might get a letter that allows you to sue in court.

The whole point of these laws is to make sure that you have the same opportunities as everyone else and that you get the support you need. Knowing your rights and speaking up when you need help can really make a big difference in your work life!

Communicating Your Needs

Communicating your needs is important in building healthy relationships, especially when managing ADHD. It is true that sometimes, it can be hard to express needs clearly. This could be because it is sometimes difficult to control your emotions; maybe you react impulsively, or fear not being understood. Mastering the skill of communicating your needs effectively creates stronger connections and greater emotional well-being. When needs aren't talked about, they often aren't met.

To communicate your needs effectively, it's important to first understand them. Take the time to think about what's missing in your relationship that makes you feel unhappy. Choosing the right time to talk about needs is also crucial. Try to pick a time when both you and your partner are calm and not stressed. Begin the conversation on a positive note. This makes your partner more willing to hear your needs. Speak about how you feel rather than what your partner is doing wrong. Be specific about your needs and invite your partner to figure out a solution together. This shows that you respect their thoughts and are willing to make a compromise.

You may fear that you'll seem too needy. It's normal to worry about this; however, everyone has needs, and talking about them means that you respect yourself and the relationship. If it's tough to clearly say what you need, writing in a journal or talking to a therapist can help. If your partner is unwilling to listen, try to stay calm and explain why the conversation is important to you. When you communicate your needs effectively, it builds a stronger foundation for your relationship.

This makes both you and your partner feel valued and understood, which creates more emotional closeness and satisfaction. It can also reduce the stress and frustration that comes from unmet needs, leading to a more peaceful and fulfilling partnership. After agreeing on changes or new behaviors, check in later to see how things are going. This shows that you're committed to improving the relationship and are paying attention to how your needs and their responses change over time.

Building a Legacy: Empowering the Next Generation of ADHD Women

You might be wondering, "Why should I worry about leaving a legacy? I'm just trying to get through today!" Well, totally understandable. But think about it this way: Your journey, your experiences, and your unique perspective can be a source of hope for others just coming up.

Building a legacy is important because it makes you a source of inspiration. Sharing your story can inspire others to overcome their own obstacles. Knowing they're not alone can make a world of difference. By connecting with other women with ADHD and sharing your experiences, you can create a supportive, strong community.

You have a role to play in advocacy. Your voice can help raise awareness about ADHD and challenge misconceptions. By sharing your story, you can help create a more inclusive society. Your legacy isn't about fame or fortune; it's about making a positive impact on the world. When you share your knowledge and experiences, you leave a lasting legacy. You also get a shot at personal growth: reflecting on your journey and sharing your story can lead to self-discovery.

Your experiences are valuable, and your story matters. Don't underestimate the power of your story to inspire and empower others. To share, start by finding a platform on which to share your journey, like Instagram, TikTok, or Twitter. Use relevant hashtags to connect with others. You can even try blogging or vlogging to share your thoughts and experiences in-depth. And if you get the chance, consider speaking at local events, conferences, or support groups.

Connect with other women with ADHD through social media groups or online forums. Trust me, sharing your experiences can be incredibly therapeutic and empowering. If you are up to the task, you could even write a book about your experiences and how you were able to deal with the challenges that surround ADHD. Lastly, you can make a long-term impact by creating (or joining) an organization dedicated to supporting women with ADHD.

Creating a Personalized ADHD Management Plan

Even for people without ADHD, life is becoming increasingly complicated. The list of appointments, bills, and subscription services might take up a full page. The best thing anyone can do to manage all of these things is to establish a clear framework and routine for as much of their daily life as possible. Creating a framework and routine shouldn't add any activities or time-consuming tasks to your day; rather, it will maximize your effectiveness in achieving the tasks you already have set out, thereby saving you both time and stress.

One of these frameworks is to make use of a calendar app like Google Calendar, Apple Calendar, etc. Schedule appointments and tasks, and set recurring reminders for daily, weekly, or monthly routines (taking meds, laundry, cleaning, etc.). I also like to add buffer time. I build an extra 10 minutes into appointments and tasks to account for distractions or unforeseen events.

Another example of a routine is: before leaving the house, do a "phone-wallet-keys" check. Develop a habit of checking your pockets for essentials before leaving the house. Assign dedicated spots for frequently used items. This reduces clutter and helps you remember where things are.

A third routine is "Start the Day Before": Prepare for the next day whenever possible. Lay out clothes, pack your bag, and prep anything you might need to avoid morning stress.

The Role of Art and Creative Expression in Managing ADHD

Art and creativity can really help with managing ADHD symptoms. It's not just about making something pretty; it's about finding a way to express yourself and focus your energy. For women with ADHD, things like painting, drawing, or sculpting can be a game-changer. It's a way to deal with intense emotions and find a safe space for self-expression.

When you're creating art, you're not just making something beautiful, you're also honing your concentration and attention to detail. That can really help with staying focused and calm, which can be a real challenge for those with ADHD.

You know how you can get impulsive sometimes? Well, art therapy naturally slows down your thought processes, helping you manage those impulses and be more thoughtful in your actions. Plus, it's a great way to regulate your emotions and find a physical outlet for stress and anxiety.

And here's the best part: completing an art project can really boost your confidence and self-esteem. It's a way to celebrate your unique talents and feel accomplished. So, incorporating art and creative expression into your self-care routine can really be transformative in managing your ADHD symptoms.

Continuing Education: Lifelong Learning Strategies for ADHD Women

Industries and technologies evolve constantly, and continuing education helps you stay updated and competitive in your field. New skills and knowledge can open doors to promotions, higher salaries, and better job opportunities.

Learning new things also challenges your mind, expands your horizons, and boosts your confidence. It can sharpen your critical thinking and problem-solving abilities, which are both valuable skills in any field.

Educational programs also offer chances to connect with like-minded individuals. Moreover, the joy of learning something new is incredibly rewarding. Continuing education can even help you prepare for a fulfilling retirement since a broader knowledge base equips you to make informed choices in life.

In spite of all these benefits, continuing education can be quite daunting. To get through it, know what works for you. Are you a visual, auditory, or kinesthetic learner? When you understand how you absorb information best, then you can choose learning methods that suit you.

Create a conducive learning environment. Find a quiet study space where you can concentrate without interruptions. A clutter-free environment can improve focus and productivity. Take breaks when you need to in order to prevent burnout and improve concentration.

Worksheet: Self-Advocacy

Create a clear and concise statement that describes your needs and how addressing them will help you succeed. This statement should be assertive yet respectful.

Example: "I need regular breaks during long meetings to help maintain my focus and productivity. This will allow me to contribute more effectively and stay engaged throughout the session."

Your Self-Advocacy Statement:

_____

_____

_____

Role play using your statement in different scenarios. You can do this with a friend, or even alone in front of a mirror. Consider how you might adapt your statement for different audiences (e.g., employers, friends, family members).

- How did it feel to say your statement aloud?
- What adjustments, if any, would you make to feel more confident?

Your Reflections:

_____

_____

_____

Think about how others might respond to your self-advocacy. Consider both supportive and challenging reactions.

- Supportive Response: "We understand and will do our best to accommodate your needs."
- Challenging Response: "We've never done that before; why do you need it?"

Your Response:

- Supportive Responses:

_____

- Challenging Responses:

_____

_____

For challenging responses, plan how you will calmly and confidently explain the importance of your needs.

Example Response Plan: "I understand this might be new, but these accommodations are crucial for me to perform at my best. I'm happy to discuss how we can make this work for both of us."

Your Response Plan:

Choose a specific situation or upcoming event where you will put your Self-Advocacy Action Plan into practice.

Your Goal:

_____

Track Your Progress: After implementing your plan, reflect on the experience.

- What worked well?
- What challenges did you encounter?
- How did you feel afterward?

Your Reflections:

- Successes:

_____

_____

-

- Challenges:

  _____

  _____

- Emotional Response:

  _____

  _____

Adjust and Improve: Based on your reflections, what changes will you make for future self-advocacy situations?

Your Adjustments:

_____

_____

_____

Create a Support Network: Identify people in your life who can support your self-advocacy efforts. This might include friends, family, colleagues, or a therapist.

Your Support Network:

_____

_____

_____

Establish a Routine: Incorporate self-advocacy into your daily or weekly routine. This could include regular check-ins with your support network or setting reminders to reassess your needs and advocacy strategies.

Your Routine Plan:

_____

_____

_____

_____

Reflection

After completing this worksheet, take a moment to reflect on how you feel about your self-advocacy journey.

- What have you learned about yourself?
- How do you feel about advocating for your needs in the future?

Your Reflection:

_____

_____

_____

Takeaways

- Some of the challenges you'll face if you've been diagnosed with ADHD are how to manage your time, start tasks, and prioritize effectively. The good news is that dialectical behavior therapy (DBT) can greatly assist you in making goal-setting more manageable.
- Advocacy is key for so many reasons. It helps you understand and communicate your needs better, which leads to healthier relationships and a more supportive environment. In your

professional life, it can help you get through challenges and ensure your contributions are valued.

- Building a legacy is important because it makes you a source of inspiration. Sharing your story can inspire others to overcome their own obstacles. Knowing they're not alone can make a world of difference.

Conclusion

Remember Kate's story? I shared a part of her story earlier (you can check the introduction). Let me tell you what became of her. Tom approached me, his face etched with a mixture of worry and hope—worry because he was losing his wife by the day, hope because he knew I could help. To say the least, being married to Kate had been very frustrating.

The once vibrant woman he'd fallen in love with seemed to have been replaced by a shadow of her former self. As he described her daily struggles, I couldn't help but see the familiar patterns of ADHD. I had first met Kate at a community event. Her energy was infectious, her laughter contagious. Yet there was an underlying restlessness, a constant need to be doing something, anything. It was during our conversation that I noticed the signs: the impulsive speech, the difficulty in focusing, and the sense of being overwhelmed.

I introduced her to dialectical behavior therapy (DBT). Although she was initially skeptical, Kate was desperate for a change. Through DBT (and most of what I have shared with you in this book), I was able to teach her skills to manage her emotions, improve communication, and get better at life generally.

Slowly but surely, a transformation started. The once chaotic household started to find its rhythm. Kate was better equipped to manage her time, prioritize tasks, and create routines. Her relationship with Tom, which was once strained by constant misunderstandings, began to heal as open communication replaced blame and resentment. She told me she found the 7 Cs of communication particularly helpful.

She also became a better mother. She gradually reduced the snapping, snarling, and yelling. Nathan's nerves got better and Henry became more open. Discipline became less about punishment and more about teaching. The house started to feel like a home.

Kate used to dread going to work, but things started to change. She learned to break big tasks into smaller ones, like eating an elephant one bite at a time. She stopped saying yes to everything and started saying no when she needed to. Gradually, she started to shine. Her boss noticed and she even got a promotion. That was a big deal—like she'd finally proven to herself that she could do it. This gave her the confidence to start her own business. It was scary, but she did it anyway.

With newfound confidence in her abilities, Kate started to see opportunities where she once saw only obstacles. She spent countless hours researching, planning, and preparing. Her ADHD, once a hindrance, became a source of creativity and innovation. She developed products and services designed to help women with ADHD get through their daily lives with greater ease. From time management tools to support groups, she built a business that reflected her own experiences and the needs of her target audience.

Launching her business was terrifying, but Kate was determined. She invested her savings, worked tirelessly, and networked with other entrepreneurs. Slowly but surely, her business started to gain traction. Customers began to share their positive experiences, and word-of-mouth spread.

The once isolated Kate now found herself surrounded by friends and colleagues who genuinely loved to be around her. Her laughter, once muffled by self-doubt, rang out freely. People loved to have her over.

Today, Kate is writing a memoir, a candid exploration of her life with ADHD. Her aim is to offer hope and guidance to others who might be struggling. Kate's story has become an inspiration to many, proving that with the right mindset and support, anyone can overcome adversity and achieve their dreams.

I understand the weight of the world that can sometimes feel like it rests squarely on your shoulders. The constant juggle of responsibilities, the internal critic, the fear of falling short—it can be overwhelming. But I want you to know that you are not alone. Many women walk this path, and while it may feel isolating, there is a sisterhood of strength and resilience waiting for you.

You might feel caught in a cycle of guilt and self-doubt. Perhaps you compare yourself to others, feeling inadequate. Or maybe the weight of expectations feels suffocating. Let me assure you, these feelings are valid. They are a part of the human experience, and you are not defined by them.

In the midst of this storm, remember you are a beloved child of God, fearfully and wonderfully made. Your worth is not determined by your accomplishments or the absence of mistakes. Your identity is rooted in His love, a love that is steadfast and unconditional.

God understands your struggles. He sees your heart, your desires, and your pain. In His Word, we find comfort and strength. "Come to me, all you who are weary and burdened, and I will give you rest. Take my yoke upon you and learn from me, for I am gentle and humble in heart, and you will find rest for your souls. For my yoke is easy and my burden is light." (Matthew 11:28-30)

This doesn't mean your challenges will disappear overnight. But it does mean you have a source of strength and resilience that surpasses human understanding. God's grace is sufficient for you.

This journey is not without its hurdles. There will be days when the weight of responsibilities feels overwhelming, and the internal critic seems louder than ever. But in these moments, remember the promises of God. He is our refuge and strength, an ever-present help in trouble (Psalm 46:1).

Can you say this word of prayer?

Dear God,

I come to You feeling overwhelmed. My mind races, thoughts scattered like leaves in a storm. I struggle to focus, to finish what I start. I feel lost, like a ship adrift at sea. Please calm the storm within me. Give me strength to get through these choppy waters. Help me to find peace in the midst of chaos.

I long for Your peace, the kind that surpasses understanding. Fill me with Your love and acceptance. Remind me of Your promises, that You are with me always, even in the darkest hours.

Guide me as I seek help and support. Give me the courage to share my struggles with others and the wisdom to accept their help.

Thank You for Your unfailing love and mercy.

In Jesus' name, I pray.

Amen.

Resources

Austin, R. D., & Pisano, G. P. (2017). Neurodiversity as a competitive advantage. *Harvard Business Review, 95*(3), 96–103.

Barkley, R. A. (1997). Behavioral inhibition, sustained attention, and executive functions: Constructing a unifying theory of ADHD. *Psychological Bulletin, 121*(1), 65–94.

Dehaene, S. (2020). *How we pay attention changes the very shape of our brains.* Literary Hub. https://lithub.com/how-we-pay-attention-changes-the-very-shape-of-our-brains/

Druskat, V. U., & Wolff, S. B. (2001). Building the emotional intelligence of groups. *Harvard Business Review*, 79(3), 80–91.

Dwyer, P. (2022). The neurodiversity approach(es): What are they and what do they mean for researchers? *Human Development, 66*(2), 73–92.

Faraone, S. V., Rostain, A. L., Blader, J., Busch, B., Childress, A. C., Connor, D. F., & Newcorn, J. H. (2019). Practitioner Review: Emotional dysregulation in attention-deficit/hyperactivity disorder—implications for clinical recognition and intervention. *Journal of Child Psychology and Psychiatry, 60*(2), 133–150.

Fuermaier, A., Tucha, L., Butzbach, M., Weisbrod, M., Aschenbrenner, S., & Tucha, O. (2021). ADHD at the workplace: ADHD symptoms, diagnostic status, and work-related functioning. *Journal of Neural Transmission, 128*(7), 1021–1031.

Gaub, M., & Carlson, C. L. (1997). Gender differences in ADHD: A meta-analysis and critical review. *Journal of the American Academy of Child & Adolescent Psychiatry, 36*(8), 1036–1045.

Hess, J. D., & Bacigalupo, A. C. (2011). Enhancing decisions and decision-making processes through the application of emotional intelligence skills. *Management Decision, 49*(5), 710–721.

Jacobs, R. L. (2001). Using human resource functions to enhance emotional intelligence. The emotionally intelligent workplace: How to select for measure, and improve emotional intelligence in individuals, groups and organizations, 159-181.

Lane, R. D., Quinlan, D. M., Schwartz, G. E., Walker, P. A., & Zeitlin, S. B. (1990). The Levels of Emotional Awareness Scale: A cognitive-developmental measure of emotion. *Journal of Personality Assessment, 55*(1-2), 124–134.

Linehan, M. M., & Wilks, C. R. (2015). The course and evolution of dialectical behavior therapy. *American Journal of Psychotherapy, 69*(2), 97–110.

Madgafurova, D. (2023). Enhancing interpersonal relationships. *Galaxy International Interdisciplinary Research Journal, 11*(11), 981–983.

Mayo Clinic Staff. (2020). *Being assertive: Reduce stress, communicate better.* Mayo Clinic.

www.mayoclinic.org/healthy-lifestyle/stress-management/in-depth/assertive/art-20044644

Millett, G., D'Amico, D., Amestoy, M. E., Gryspeerdt, C., & Fiocco, A. J. (2021). Do group-based mindfulness meditation programs enhance executive functioning? A systematic review and meta-analysis of the evidence. *Consciousness and Cognition, 95*, 103195.

Mind Tools Content Team. (n.d.) *The 7 Cs of communication.* MindTools. https://www.mindtools.com/a5xap8q/the-7-cs-of-communication

Rizvi, S. L., Steffel, L. M., & Carson-Wong, A. (2013). An overview of dialectical behavior therapy for professional psychologists. *Professional Psychology: Research and Practice, 44*(2), 73–80.

Robins, C. J., & Rosenthal, M. Z. (2011). Dialectical behavior therapy. In J. D. Herbert & E. M. Forman (eds), *Acceptance and mindfulness in cognitive behavior therapy: Understanding and applying the new therapies,* 164–192.

Rosqvist, H. B., Chown, N., & Stenning, A. (2020). *Neurodiversity studies.* Routledge.

Rowland, A. S., Lesesne, C. A., & Abramowitz, A. J. (2002). The epidemiology of attention-deficit/hyperactivity disorder (ADHD): A public health view. *Mental Retardation and Developmental Disabilities Research Reviews, 8*(3), 162–170.

Richelieu, D. (2024). Self-esteem among adults with ADHD symptoms. *Walden Dissertations and Doctoral Studies*, 15521.

Schwartz, P. (1997). *Art of the long view: Planning for the future in an uncertain world.* John Wiley & Sons.

Sedgwick, J. A., Merwood, A., & Asherson, P. (2019). The positive aspects of attention deficit hyperactivity disorder: A qualitative investigation of successful adults with ADHD. *ADHD Attention Deficit and Hyperactivity Disorders, 11*(3), 241–253.

Stein, D. J., & Harvey, B. A. "The compulsive-impulsive spectrum and behavioral addictions," in J. E. Grant and M. N. Potenza (eds), *The Oxford Handbook of Impulse Control Disorders*, Oxford Library of Psychology (2011).

TEDx Talks. (2020, January 24). *How to eliminate self doubt forever & the power of your unconscious mind | Peter Sage | TEDxPatras* [Video]. YouTube. https://www.youtube.com/watch?v=v1ojZKWfShQ

Tsotsos, J. K. (2019). Attention: The messy reality. *The Yale Journal of Biology and Medicine, 92*(1), 127–137.

Weisberg, O., GalOz, A., Berkowitz, R., Weiss, N., Peretz, O., Azoulai, S., KoplemanRubin, D., & Zuckerman, O. (2014). TangiPlan: Designing an assistive technology to enhance executive functioning among children with ADHD. *Proceedings of the 2014 Conference on Interaction Design and Children*, 293–296.

Printed in Great Britain
by Amazon